PRACTICAL COMMUNICATION FOR MANAGERS

by Barry Maude

Longman

London and New York

LONGMAN GROUP LIMITED
London

Associated companies, branches and representatives
throughout the world

Published in the United States of America by
Longman Inc., New York

First published 1974
Third impression 1978

ISBN 0 582 41046.0 Paper

Library of Congress Catalog Card Number 73-92008

Set in IBM Press Roman 10/11 pt by
Santype Ltd. (Coldtype Division)
Salisbury, Wiltshire
and printed in Hong Kong by
Wing King Tong Printing Co Ltd

Preface

What a tremendous boost there would be in your managerial performance if only you could find ways of improving your communication ability. *The techniques described in this book could lead to such improvements.*

Future generations of managers may be able to solve their problems by using mathematical symbols, but at present most management problems have to be thought out and fought out in words. So this book deals with language – speaking it, writing it, listening to it, using it in meetings.

But not all communication problems can be solved by word of mouth or pen so several other important aspects of communication are covered. These include information needs, communication barriers, and the use of media.

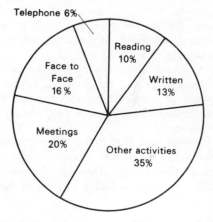

Fig. 1: *Communicating takes up more of the manager's time at work than any other activity. This chart shows the average percentage of the working day spent in various activities by managers in a large construction company in the Midlands.*

One of the main barriers to communication is the ambiguity of the term itself. For the word has been stretched across vast areas which include psychology, sociology, linguistics, information theory, mass media studies and small group studies. Hundreds of academic texts have been written for the specialist, examining particular aspects in minute detail. But this book is for the manager or management student whose interest in the subject is mainly practical and who wants the overall picture rather than the big close-up.

Most managers are intensely pragmatic in their approach to problems, perhaps because the realities of their jobs – the time-pressures, the crises, the bewildering rate of change – force them to solve most of their problems *quickly* and by rule of thumb. In the real-time world of management there is little room for the complicated concepts and models in which some management writers seem to specialise. That is why this book avoids generality and abstraction and tries, instead, to provide practical hints and techniques – the kind that managers can apply in their own jobs.

Many people have contributed to make this book possible. I am grateful to colleagues and students in the Management Department of the North Staffordshire Polytechnic for helping to clarify many of the issues dealt with here; to Dr J. Schermer for contributing a chapter on the important subject of communication between managers from different countries; to Dr K. Wisdom in Australia for sustaining a long-distance dialogue about the manuscript; and to Ian Woolf of BBC Television's Further Education department for helping to clarify many of the points discussed in Chapter 12.

I should like to thank Dave Spall for his valuable advice about modern printing technology and for providing figures 25 and 26; and also Derek Halfpenny of Josiah Wedgwoods for providing much useful information about house journals, I am particularly grateful to my wife, Mollie, for much patience.

Some of the material used here first appeared in article form, and I should like to thank the following magazines for permission to use it again: *Industrial & Commercial Training, Management in Action, Management Today, Supervisory Management, The Accountant, Times Educational Supplement.*

Contents

1 Managing by Meeting

'Some committees are distinguished only for the non-meeting of minds.'

Today, meetings are big business. Group participation is in vogue and the wheels of modern industry are turned by committees. Yet according to one expert only one meeting in ten works efficiently. This chapter examines some of the reasons why and suggests some remedies.

When, after years of gentle stagnation, a company's production goes through the roof it is sometimes on the strength of a single new idea which has exploded in the board room: group participation. Scott Bader and Landsmans, for instance, have chalked up much higher sales per worker since they opted for co-ownership and the group approach that goes with it. No doubt many more firms could achieve zippier growth if only they dared to experiment with this modern alchemy.

Autocratic management methods may flatter the egos of a few top men. But just how frustrating they can be for everyone else many a loss-laden annual report shows. Everybody needs status, not just the tycoons, and the most telling measure of status is the right to share in decisions. One psychiatrist has even laid the current crime wave at the battered door of the autocratic manager. According to Dr Roger Tredgold, thousands of people who only find soul-destroying boredom in their jobs look for physical outlets in the shape of hooliganism, demonstrations and violence.

Certainly anyone who has squirmed beneath the thumb of an occupational dictator will cheer on those companies which have thrust forward to more participative styles of management. More and more companies seem to be doing so. No doubt the trend reflects the increase in the number of specialists in organisations. Another reason may be that industrial organisation has become too big for the single decision-maker. Thus even firms in the grip of a strong man have their informal committees, with managers meeting over coffee to discuss production or marketing problems, and supervisors chatting in the canteen about new safety practices or overtime schedules. And in even the most autocratic firm at least one formal committee operates – the board of directors.

Group process in modern business

A major symptom of the new approach is group discussion, which aims to make more efficient use of people as well as of machinery. This was the effect achieved at Boeing in 1972 during a serious slump. Top managers began to meet for a few hours each day, the idea being to pool new ideas and knowledge so that ways of stimulating new business could be identified. As a result of these meetings proposals emerged which led the company to explore new approaches to *land* and *water* transportation. These new approaches helped to pull the company out of its nose dive.

You still hear the wisecracks – a meeting is a meeting to decide when the next meeting will be held; a meeting comprises a group of the unfit appointed by the unwilling to do the unnecessary. But the fact is that today a company's personnel and production policies, its marketing plans, its advertising schedules, are almost certain to be thrashed out in meetings. The wheels of modern industry are turned by committees. There are finance committees, joint consultative committees, progress meetings, supervisors' meetings, staff conferences. . . . How many thousands of meetings like this are held each day in Britain?

Group discussion plays a vital role in modern business. That is why the minimum communication programme of many large companies includes:

• *General Manager's meetings*, held quarterly, say, by the General Manager with managers reporting to him, with the aim of reviewing progress and talking about future plans. Varied expert knowledge and experience can be brought to bear on complex problems.

• *Staff meetings* held monthly, say, by each senior manager with his juniors so as to bridge gaps between managerial levels. Junior executives are developed for higher responsibility by participating in assignments which may stem from these meetings.

• *Supervisors' meetings* held at regular intervals. Supervisors meet with their work teams to discuss plans, progress and problems.

Meetings like these serve many purposes. They may be used for briefing subordinates, for creative problem-solving or to help a manager to make a correct decision.

Three reasons for training yourself in committee skills

Here are three good reasons why the manager needs to take committee work seriously and train himself in the relevant skills:

1. *Group discussion is one of the most powerful tools of persuasion.* A manager experienced in the ways that committees work can persuade people to think again and get plans and changes accepted where his less experienced colleagues fail. Bavelas found that lecturing, ordering or appealing to workers were ineffective ways of stimulating a production-rise: but production rose steadily once a group decision had been reached.

2. *Being involved in meetings sharpens people's feelings for the business as a whole.* They are therefore continually being developed for more responsible jobs in the firm. 'Serving on committees,' one executive reported, 'forces me to organise my own thinking about what goes on in this company, and to dig up facts to support the conclusions I reach.'

3. *Subordinates willingly support decisions which they have had a hand in making.* That is why even those executives who think they can reach better decisions acting alone often value meetings. Also they know that their own boss is more likely to accept decisions arrived at by group participation.

In the past the exploited many have sweated for the idle few. In the future the masses will grow fat and lazy with leisure while a corps of top executives works overtime. It is the wise manager who feels the way the wind is blowing and, deciding against ulcers, leaves some of the decisions to his committee colleagues. It is the indispensable man who can make himself dispensable.

Why committees creak

Jot down the main disadvantages of the meetings you attend and your list will probably look something like this:

- Meetings consume time yet often fail to produce good decisions.
- Some meetings are an organised pooling of ignorance.
- Often the wrong people seem to attend.
- Meetings breed compromise solutions which nobody completely supports.
- Committees weaken the autonomy of departments.

Moreover, many meetings are a terrible waste of talent. The consensus-seeking machinery of the committee, the reduction of all policy to a common denominator, can result in a terrible dull dreariness. A committee can be a cul-de-sac into which ideas are lured and then quietly strangled.

Sometimes a committee seems to act merely as an instrument for an official who reads its letters and writes its replies ('The X Committee requires me to point out that . . .').

He holds up the committee as a vague body which would be 'reluctant' to do this or would be 'unhappy' about that; a body which 'had not contemplated acting on these lines' . . . In this way citizens are held back from the committee . . . so as to avoid holding up the administrative processes which the official is carrying out.[1]

There is much evidence that tells the same tale: that many organisations are wasting vast amounts of time and money because of badly run meetings. Consultant James Rice, for instance, has studied meetings in a hundred large firms and he reckons that no more than one meeting in ten works efficiently. According to Rice many meetings should never be called at all — the items could be better dealt with by normal administrative means. And when the Ansul Chemical Company

[1] K. C. Wheare, *Government by Committee*, Oxford University Press, 1955.

took a critical look at how well its meetings were working it found that the wrong sort of people often seemed to attend.[1]

When committees are distinguished only for the non-meeting of minds the responsibility for revitalising them surely lies with top management. The Board of the Ansul Chemical Company accepted this responsibility and trained its executives in the formal aspects of committee work and in dealing with the psychological factors. Dramatic improvements followed. Meetings got more accomplished in the same time. Perhaps more companies should provide training of this kind.

Problems and Solutions

Problem	Possible solutions
1. Company meetings are a waste of time. Results fail to justify the expense.	A senior manager reviews each committee every year to decide if its terms of reference need changing, if its membership needs changing, and if work is being handled which could be better dealt with by the regular administrative machine.
2. Often the wrong sort of people seem to attend company meetings. Result: poor idea-production and low-quality decisions.	Invite an outside observer into meetings – e.g. a consultant with knowledge of <u>sociometric techniques</u>. The committee will be able to discuss its methods and performance with him at the end of meetings. The consultant will be able to tell you:

      · who is aggressive and domineering
      · who makes positive or negative contributions
      · who the information-givers are and who the opinion-givers are
      · who the morale-boosters are
      · who would make the best chairman
      · who should leave the committee and what type of new people should be brought in.

[1] Hoffman found that groups made up of people of unlike personality produce better solutions than like-minded people. South and Gurnee both found that single-sex committees are more efficient than mixed.

3. Company meetings are very expensive.

A single meeting can cost the company hundreds or thousands of pounds. So hold a meeting only if the results will justify the expense – i.e. if there is no cheaper way of handling the problem adequately.

You want to test opinion about a possible switch to a two-shift system. You consider calling a meeting. But, being cost-conscious, you eventually decide to draft some proposals instead and circulate these for comment. When drawing up the final details you take account of any remarks made by your colleagues. Result: similar product – lower cost.

4. Company meetings are slow and badly run.

Ask the committee to find ways of streamlining its performance. Train committee chairmen and secretaries in the appropriate skills – this should straighten out most of the kinks. There may be suitable courses run locally, otherwise you may have to bring in an outside expert.

5. There is too much conflict in meetings.

Arrange T-Group training for committee members.[1] Bunker discovered lasting behaviour in some executives as a result of T-Group training including (*a*) more effort to understand and listen to others, (*b*) more tact and tolerance, (*c*) less willingness to make snap judgments.

Optimum size of meetings

A well-trained committee can be the hottest horse in the manager's stable, but only if it carries the right weight. Meetings which are too big or too small don't work well – as Fig. 3 shows. The precise number

[1] The T-Groups run by Leeds University and by the Tavistock Institute of Human Relations have won a high reputation. Both are usually oversubscribed.

Assessing committee effectiveness*

Ineffective	Effective
1 Conflict Avoidance through suppression and compromise.	Acceptance and working through of conflict.
2 Discipline Controls imposed. Restrictive and conformist environment.	Controls self-imposed. Free and tolerant environment.
3 Communication Guarded, cautious communication. Mutual suspicion.	Full and free communication. Mutual trust.
4 Team spirit Self-seeking; individualist.	General concern for each other.
5 Human resources Little use of individual talents.	Full use of individual talents.
6 Efficiency Haphazard or circular progression in meetings. Irrational or low-quality decisions often made.	Committee thinks straight and logically; sound decisions made.

*Adapted from scales by Douglas McGregor and John Paul Jones.

Fig. 2: *Completing a rating scale of this kind and studying the results enables a committee to see which aspects of their performance need strengthening. Knowing their weaknesses they are better equipped to improve their overall performance.*

must be based on knowledge of the people concerned and of the problem, and on other local factors. But, in very general terms, the optimum size for a meeting seems to be between five and ten. In groups of this size people can talk nearly as much as they want to and exert influence over each other. Yet there is sufficient variety of talent and experience to tackle problems imaginatively. Groups of this size require only minimal effort to organise themselves and it is possible to assimilate each man's thinking into the final decision.

Seashore concluded that the larger the group the greater the difficulty it had in becoming a cohesive and effective unit — a finding supported by Gibb and also Revans. Moede observed members of a group who pulled a rope as hard as possible. At intervals an extra man was added to the team. With each increase in membership there was a decreased average contribution by each member.

As the size of a meeting goes up the amount of satisfaction felt by members goes down. Bales found that as meetings get larger more and more communication is directed to one member — there is less general interaction. Moreover, large groups split into subgroups and waste much time on procedure.[1]

In a large unstructured committee a small cell, voting as a block, can dominate proceedings. According to Penrose the number required is the square root of the total number attending.

The Laboratory of Social Relations at Harvard which has been investigating problems of this kind since 1947, has concluded that five is the ideal number for a problem-solving meeting. While H. Bonner concludes, after a detailed examination of the whole question of size: 'Groups consisting of six to ten persons offer maximum conditions for interaction in group problem-solving.'

Optimum size of meetings

2-man meetings	3-man meetings	4-man meetings
Impractical. Biased or freakish decisions are likely. Each person can exercise a complete veto over the other.	The tendency is for two members to unite against the third. The odd man out is likely to withdraw into himself (stop being productive) or set up a damaging protest movement. And three-man meetings lack the error correcting characteristics of larger groups.	Sharp cleavages tend to appear — three against one or two against two. Meetings of this size may have insufficient breadth of experience and are too lacking in variety and intellectual stimulus to produce good results.
5–10 members	**Over 10 members**	**Over 15 members**
In meetings of this size people can talk nearly as much as they want to and exert influence over each other. There is sufficient variety of talent and personality to tackle problems imaginatively. Groups of this size offer good conditions for interaction and therefore for group problem-solving.	As the group grows in numbers an increasing number of people are scared into silence. Intimate face-to-face contact becomes difficult and the group may split into cliques.	Low participators stop talking to each other and either stay silent or talk only to the few top men. Thus interaction — and creativity — freeze. Yet big groups can solve certain kinds of problem more efficiently than smaller groups* — e.g. where there is a correct and verifiable answer (the cheapest method of erecting a fence or building a cycle shed). The more people in the meeting the more chance that it contains an expert who knows the answer.

* Gordon found that the larger the group the more accurate was its estimate of the weights of objects: errors tend to cancel each other out in accordance with statistical laws.

Fig. 3: *This chart shows the strengths and weaknesses of meetings of varying sizes.*

[1] 'The maximum size of an effective unit is limited by the ability of that unit to solve its problems of internal communication,' Simon, Smithburg and Thompson, 1959.

Meetings are big business

A report in the *Harvard Business Review* reveals the importance of meetings to American executives — no doubt a similar pattern prevails in British companies. After examining replies to a questionnaire sent to subscribers the journal reported:

> Mr Average Executive spends nearly 3½ hours a week in committee meetings; serves on three committees . . . finds an average of seven fellow executives sitting with him on each committee, and wishes there were only four others. Generally, each of his committees meets about every two weeks.
>
> In addition to these formal committee meetings, he spends the equivalent of one working day a week . . . in informal conference and consultation with fellow executives. . . .
>
> Committees are considered important devices for sharing information, cross-fertilising ideas, and promoting coordinated management. While there are some executives who would allow committees to vote decisions and make policy, there are many more who prefer that committees recommend and advise the executive held responsible for the decision — frequently the chairman of the committee.

Meetings are big business these days. And every manager needs a good knowledge of the techniques for successfully running them and participating in them. Some of these techniques are outlined in the next three chapters.

Some questions

1. What are the advantages of arriving at decisions by group participation?
2. How can a committee be trained to improve its performance?
3. Often the wrong people seem to attend committee meetings: how could you ensure that the right people were attending?
4. What is the optimum size for a problem-solving meeting?
5. What are the main disadvantages of large meetings?

2 The Hot Seat

'The temptation is to respond to aggression with aggression.'

Every manager needs to master the skills of chairmanship: without them his value to the company is reduced and he may never rise to the position that, in all other ways, he merits. Arguably, the key to good chairmanship is flexibility. The good chairman is a man who assesses the kind of leadership that a particular meeting requires then adjusts his style accordingly. Equally important is his ability to deal with conflict and other psychological factors: and to control and guide the discussion.

Group leadership goes to the man who best fits the occasion. At normal times this may be the steady man. In a wildcat strike the awkward aggressive man may emerge as leader. In Bion's study of groups of neurotics during the war often it was the man with the most problems who led the group. Insane or neurotic politicians are catapulted into leadership in convulsive periods of history. The small expanding company and the national corporation need quite different kinds of chairman. .

You don't learn good chairmanship by studying a list of do's and don't's. For the good leader is not a man with a string of adjectives like impartial and decisive after his name. In companies, leadership is no longer thought of as a set of permanent qualities enabling one man to march others smartly through the business jungle. The leader is the man who fits the situation. The born leader in one situation may be reduced to stumbling ineffectuality in another. Josephine Klein sees leadership as the ability to elicit the right response, and this may require the gentle touch, even self-effacement.

Leadership is impermanent and shifting. Imagine six men in a meeting. One offers a suggestion and the others start listening. The six become a group focused on the man with the possible solution, who momentarily becomes the leader. Once his suggestion is accepted the group goal changes and members wait for another momentary leader to emerge.[1]

The good chairman is a man who, at the beginning of a meeting, can size up the situation, decide what kind of leadership is required, then adjust his style accordingly. In one meeting he is quiet and self-effacing – a kind of idea-eunuch, deliberately witholding his intellectual virility. But he becomes a tough, fast-talking overlord at the next meeting. Each style exhibits leadership if it is right for the occasion.

Today the chairman is a suction-pump drawing out members' ideas. Tomorrow he becomes a conveyor-belt, feeding the group with information, carrying them speedily and efficiently towards a decision.

Vary your style

So by discreet use of the loud and soft pedals you become a man for all meetings. Basically there are only five or six reasons for holding a meeting:

- to inform
- to collect information and opinions
- to solve problems, make decisions
- to negotiate
- to coordinate and control

[1] My own experience suggests that when a committee first meet they select the most *talkative* person as leader; he helps them to forget their uncertainty and insecurity. As they get to know each other those who contribute most to the task are usually recognised and selected as leaders.

Low-level meetings tend to be informational in aim; while high-level meetings tend more to decision-making and problem-solving. To win your chairman's good-conduct medal you need first to identify correctly the kind of meeting it is and then to bring the appropriate style of chairmanship into play.

Imagine you have three meetings booked for next week: they have different objectives so will require different approaches. But as chairman you will act as a catalyst on each occasion and help the meeting to attain the structure that is most suitable for its purpose:

Monday.   You explain the effects of a forthcoming company merger to your staff. You know the facts, they don't – so you do most of the talking. You remain in firm control throughout and rightly limit staff participation to a question-and-answer session at the end. As they punch the knowledge-box you respond with facts and advice.

Tuesday.   You call together some junior managers to decide how to reduce the high rate of staff turnover. You provide the participants with broad alternatives but leave them to make the final choice of method: they will have to implement any decision so it had better be one which commands their full support.[1] You keep the meeting small – no more than six or seven – so as to get maximum interaction, and you try to establish a free, informal atmosphere so that the ideas will flow. You impose only as much structure as will ensure that *all* aspects of the problem are examined.

Friday.   Some technicians come to see you with a shopping list of grievances ranging from holiday arrangements to overtime schedules. Recognising that the purpose of this meeting is therapeutic, your main aim is to provide opportunities for the men to express their feelings. You recognise that any decision taken will be less important than the emotional release it provides. So you adopt a democratic style, try to establish a permissive atmosphere so that the men will feel free to say exactly what is on their minds. Such an atmosphere is best achieved with no leader at all. So you sit with the men around the table and deliberately refrain from controlling the discussion. Instead you allow leadership to be taken over by different men at different times.

If, by some gross miscalculation, you had included all three topics – the merger, staff turnover and the grievances – on the agenda of the

[1] The great danger of delegating decision-making in this way is that your subordinates may take a decision with which you don't agree but for which you stay responsible in the eyes of your own boss.

same meeting, then you would have needed to change your style as you moved from one topic to the other.

Remember, though, that in command meetings (i.e. meetings called at the boss's discretion and attended by subordinates) the manager who calls the meeting is really making the decisions, whatever the procedure used. As Wilfred Brown has pointed out, if the manager accepts the majority view than his acceptance automatically makes the decision his own. Management philosophy is that the person held accountable for a decision should be the one who makes it.

Control of meetings

Purpose of meeting	*Control method*
1 Giving or exchanging information	Highly structured, authoritarian leadership. Controlled participation. Little interaction. Chairman stays at the centre of the discussion.
2 Making policy	The chairman keeps as much control as is needed to coordinate and collate members' ideas. He may decide to move the discussion through a pre-planned sequence to ensure that all relevant aspects are covered in the time available. **Main aim:** to arrive at a high-quality decision. **Important secondary aim:** to make the decision as representative as possible.
3 Problem-solving	The amount of structure to be imposed depends on the type of problem. Generally, unstructured problems ('How could we expand the business?') benefit from an unstructured approach and a 'democratic' style of chairmanship. In such meetings the chairman controls proceedings only to the extent necessary to protect members from criticism and to deal with conflict.
4 Cathartic (e.g. expression of grievances)	Unstructured. Participants allowed to interact spontaneously and to contribute at will. The chairman tries to establish a permissive atmosphere while himself remaining in the background. The type of decision taken is less important than its acceptability to the participants.

Fig. 4:

13

Free or Controlled Discussion?

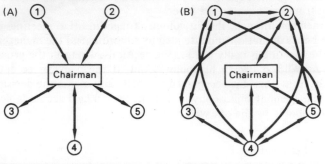

Fig. 5: *Should the chairman remain at the centre of the discussion (A) or allow the members to interact freely (B)? An experienced chairman varies his style to match the purpose of the meeting.*

The hidden agenda

Experts such as Edgar Schein and W. R. Bion have identified the most common forms of emotional behaviour in meetings:

Flight: avoiding facing the crucial issue and possible conflict by too-eagerly accepting compromise.

Fight: conflict between members which doesn't spring from disagreements about the topic being debated.

Dependency: on the leader or another person, thus seeking to avoid responsibility for making decisions.

Pairing, which indicates a striving for emotional security.

Withdrawal as a way of escaping tension and conflict or feelings of inadequacy. Often this results in passive and bland behaviour and arguments that feelings have no place in meetings and should be ruled out of order.

Emotional responses like these can interfere with the real work of the meeting and it is your duty as chairman to counteract or neutralise them so that the meeting can get on with its business. Thus your ability to deal with feelings is a key skill.

The Group Dynamics approach – with which, in this country, the Tavistock Institute is closely associated – assumes that people interact at two levels, the rational and the irrational; i.e. the level of what *seems* to be said and decided and the *unspoken* level of fears, power- and

Discussion Leadership

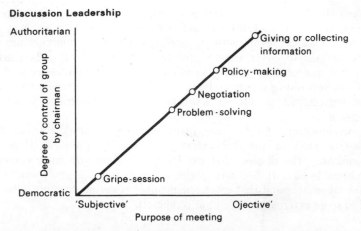

Fig. 6: *A democratic style is right when the purpose of the meeting is 'subjective' — i.e. when quality of decision is less important than acceptability. An authoritarian chairman makes quick decisions possible but much time may be spent later in explaining and winning support for those decisions.*

status-seeking, rivalry and so on. The two levels are revealed in this scene from Doris Lessing's novel, *A Ripple from the Storm*:

> Boris Krueger stood up from somewhere in the middle of the packed hall and proposed that the society should produce a book consisting of articles about Russia ... The faction represented by Messrs Perr, Forester and Pyecroft said that to sell a book of articles would be interpreted as making propaganda about Russia. The faction represented by Krueger, Anto Hesse and Andrew McGrew said it would be purely factual and nothing to do with propaganda. *The real battle was over who was to control this society.* That there was a battle was not understood by the respectable patrons, who did not attend the committee meetings. Since the committee could not agree, the battle was to be fought out now by the membership. Boris Krueger's proposal was the flinging down of a gauge in public ... listening to the words people use is the longest way around to an understanding of what is going on.[1]

In most meetings the members are grappling not only with topics on the agenda but also with these irrational, 'hidden agenda' items: secret

[1] (Michael Joseph, 1958) Panther edn., p. 13. Author's italics added.

power struggles, jealousies and anxieties, hidden fears and aggressions. These emotional factors can have a profound effect on the way in which topics are dealt with in meetings, where the common use of English fails to cover the frightening psychological gaps. Too little emotion in a meeting is bad — a certain degree of tension is necessary to get the best out of a person. But too much emotion is equally bad, and can overcommit people to a wrong line of argument or a wrong decision.

An observer who has seen many meetings at work through the one-way glass at the Laboratory of Social Relations at Harvard, comments: 'The illusion that the group is dealing with some external problem breaks. It becomes perfectly transparent . . . that emotions have taken over and that what one member is saying does not refer at all to some external situation but to himself.'

Dealing with aggression

When, as chairman, you find yourself trapped in the middle of emotional crossfire your best tactic is to encourage the snipers to fire blanks. Help people to express their feelings in harmless ways for until this expression of emotions has happened they will stand in the way of the committee's work. So:

1. Listen to the angry objector with the attitude of withholding judgment and wishing only to understand what he means. Each member is constantly looking for signs of approval or disapproval: his anger may merely be a minor demonstration against the group's lack of understanding.
2. Restate his thoughts in other words to make sure the other members understand.
3. Show that you are willing to explore his objections fully. You thus provide the security he probably needs. If he is attacked or ignored he may withdraw into himself or start sniping at others.

A tolerant approach by the chairman relaxes the tension and gives the objector a chance of adjusting his own attitude instead of driving him into a tight defensive corner. At one meeting I attended the chairman handled just this kind of situation with great skill. An Education Committee meeting was being held at the time of the postal strike in 1971. The committee agreed that in cases of hardship the children of strikers should be entitled to free school meals, clothing grants and other forms of assistance. A member of the committee lost his temper:

Chairman: We're all agreed then?

Member: No, we're not all agreed. It's no use trying to steamroller us like this.

> (*At this point a less experienced chairman might have reacted angrily – 'Who says I'm trying to steamroller you?' But instead he encouraged the member to express his feelings.*)

Chairman: Are you objecting to our helping the children of strikers, or do you simply object to this kind of assistance?

Member: If people go on strike it's their own lookout. It's no use striking then shouting out because your children need clothes. We've no right to spend public money like this.

> (*The chairman might have thrown in counter-arguments at this stage, sharpening the conflict. Instead he showed a willingness to hear the man out.*)

Chairman: You think that any hardship experienced by these children is solely the parents' responsibility?

Member: Yes I do. We've no right to use the rate-payers' money to subsidise strikes.

> (*Now the chairman tried to make the speaker specify exactly what he wouldn't accept, so drawing him away from the emotional concept of 'strikes'.*)

Chairman: Are you proposing that we should provide no assistance at all for these children? Are you against allowing them free school dinners?

Member: No, I'm not saying that. We may have to provide dinners . . .

Already the objector was adjusting his position because of the chairman's handling of the situation. The temptation is, of course, to respond to aggression with aggression – for instance, by producing crushing counterarguments or simply shutting the man up. But such retaliatory behaviour only deepens the conflict or, at best, postpones trouble until later. When everybody is stoking the boiler your job as chairman is to keep the safety valves open: 'Permitting and exploring emotional expressions will lead to initial discomfort but will, in the long run, produce a higher level of communication and a stronger, more effective group'.[1]

---

[1] E. H. Schein; *Process Consultation: its role in organisational development* (Addison Wesley, 1969) p. 37.

Thus it may not be possible to launch into problem-solving at once. As Edgar Schein has observed, the early stages of a new committee are a period of essentially self-oriented behaviour, the members being preoccupied with problems of influence and status, choosing a role, and so on. Unless the chairman allows a period for emotional growth the group will be unable to get to grips with its task. Thus, especially in the early stages of a committee's life, irrational, emotional behaviour plays a *constructive* role.

By being aware of members' personal needs and by encouraging them to bring their feelings into the opening by attentive listening and skilful questioning, you may be able to help the group to 'find itself', to relieve its inner tensions, and so create the conditions for a series of successful meetings.

Harnessing conflict

Too much agreement in a meeting is not a good sign. For there are always some ideas that are so unsuitable that not to disagree means not to solve the problem. A lot of agreement may show lack of involvement or an inhibiting atmosphere. A team of Harvard researchers have found that in most meetings there are about half as many negative as positive contributions — a kind of optimum balance. And the conflict need not be crude and obvious. It can be so subtle that only the experienced know it's there. On the surface all may be sweetness and light. But if you listen carefully you can hear the sound of heavy artillery in the distance. A tone of voice, a brief silence, a polite question, can wreak havoc in the enemy camp.

But when there is too much conflict, when people stop listening and start seeing eye to eye because they are shouting in each other's faces, then at least make sure they are disagreeing about a real issue and not a whirl of air. For many disagreements in meetings are semantic, simply spun out of words:

A: There's a damn sight too much spending on welfare in this company.
B: Nonsense! Welfare is a very important item. It's essential for morale. We need to spend more not less . . .

He pauses for breath — you slip in smartly and ask each man to restate his position clearly so that there's no misunderstanding. You invite each man to give *specific examples*:

Chairman: I think this is an important point – what sort of items would you like to cut back on, Mr A?

A: Well there's the sports club which gets a £5000 subsidy – but only a handful of people ever use it.

Chairman: Is that the sort of item you'd like to spend *more* on, Mr B?

B: Not exactly. I was thinking more of functions like the children's Christmas party.

A: Well I wouldn't take issue with you over the Christmas party. . . .

The fire burns out. The committee's work goes on.

Permit conflict and disagreement to be acted out as it arises. Relieve the inner tensions of the group by the sort of skilful questioning and active listening that brings feelings out into the open. Don't rebuke or squash the rude, aggressive man: instead invite him to say why he disagrees. However, don't let grown men quarrel over generalisations, which are mere words. Make them specify.

Properly handled, conflict can be used to increase the range of alternative proposals. And if there is genuine disagreement over a real issue the resulting tussle may serve to shape a superior solution.

When faced with crisis the group may suppress conflict within its own ranks and instead project aggressive feelings onto outsiders. Two groups are brought into a room; red name tags and pens are given to one group, green to the other. The groups then complete questionnaires in sight of each other, but there is no interaction. Within minutes each group experiences defensive feelings and fear of the other group. In another experiment, two groups are given a task and told that a jury will assess the results. In less than an hour each group has developed into a tightly knit band, regards its product as excellent and the other group's as poor or mediocre. 'They' becomes 'enemy'.

Three ways of reducing your authority

A high-ranking individual in a meeting usually has a dominating influence. People defer to him. Even if he doesn't speak members try to interpret his silences. Result: an expensive kind of one-man decision-making. In many business meetings the chairman is the most high-ranking individual present and he exercises a strong control over other members (a) by his authority as boss, (b) by framing and defining the problem initially, and (c) by controlling participation. The resulting atmosphere is usually authoritarian, which is all right so long as this atmosphere creates the conditions for successful problem-solving but all wrong if an informal atmosphere would produce better results. Guetzkow has observed that programmed, repetitive tasks can be efficiently disposed of in meetings which have much 'structure' and are run by authoritarian methods; while more wide-open patterns are more suitable for tackling less structured tasks.

Think back to the last meeting that you chaired:

· Was there enough free interaction in the meeting?
· Did you have the impression that people felt free to speak their minds?
· Did their comments make much impression on you?
· Were any of the recommendations made by the members actually implemented?
· Did junior members continuously defer to seniors?

The answers to these questions will tell you whether your meeting suffered from the 'authority effect', which inhibits the discussion, blocks free communication and silences lower-status members. The following techniques can help to reduce this effect:

1. *Chair rotation.* Each member takes turn to be chairman. Prince has noted[1] that this technique adds a vital interest to meetings (most meetings need it!), besides testing and developing each man's expertise. Members are motivated to stay with an idea, to be positive in approach and to cooperate with the present chairman: for each member knows he'll soon be in the hot seat himself and needing all the support he can get — including the support of past chairmen. Through chair rotation juniors get their chance to lead and generally the atmosphere is relaxed and the talk unrestrained.

2. *Chairman reticence.* The chairman contributes his own opinions only *after* all other ideas have been explored so that people are not constantly trying either to please or to counter the boss. When the chairman talks too much and too early the discussion may become a series of reactions to his ideas, pro and con, so that many valuable ideas never hatch out of the egg. It also helps if the chairman deliberately comes to the meeting with an open mind and allows his own opinion to form only after hearing what everybody else thinks.

[1] G. Prince, 'Towards better meetings', *Harvard Business Review*, Jan.–Feb. 1969.

3. *Sitting out silences.* After the chairman's opening statement and explanation of the problem there is often a build-up of tension and a general reluctance to speak — perhaps because members are anxious to find out where other people stand before they commit themselves. Or they hope that someone will accept responsibility for guiding the meeting and lead them down the right path. Whatever the reason, they often sit there with their mouths shut. Many inexperienced chairmen plunge nervously into this opening silence, suggest ways of tackling the problem and find themselves controlling and directing the meeting in a way they never intended. The most effective antidote is mentally to refuse to accept responsibility for getting the meeting moving: instead, throw this responsibility onto the members themselves. Don't try to solve the problem by yourself — if this had been the rational thing to do you wouldn't have called the meeting. So sit there in silence with them until somebody else speaks. Sitting it out is wearing on the nerves, but worth while if members emerge from the test with an increased sense of responsibility.

Another reason for sitting it out is that silence can be positive and creative. After minutes of complete silence there can be a sudden flash, a new cross-fertilising of ideas, and the hidden factor leaps from somebody's lips.

The findings of the National Industrial Conference Board show that the most common pitfalls in business meetings are caused by leader-dominance and especially when

· the chairman talks too much himself
· the chairman inhibits free discussion by leading questions and suggestions
· the chairman keeps the meeting going too fast and fails to give the group time to develop its own solution.

Thus in meetings where a free, informal atmosphere is desirable your first duty as chairman is to dilute your own influence, restrain your own comments, let others speak first. Your last duty, at the end of the meeting, may well be to hand office to someone else. As a result creativity should improve. For consciousness of authority and status blocks free communication, lowers the contribution of low-status members and makes them less likely to learn. Another effect is that high-status criticise low-status members but fail to criticise each other.

Five Reasons for Reducing the Chairman's Authority

5. The chairman may unconsciously cultivate an ear for comments that echo his own predjudices and give them preference

4. Performance of junior members goes down: they tend to undervalue their own contributions.

3. Members soon take the measure of the chairman-boss and shape their contributions according to what they think he wants to hear.

2. Idea-production goes down (the company pays the bill).

1. Communication is choked. People don't feel free to speak their minds in an authoritarian atmosphere.

Fig. 7: *To steer the committee around these dangers the chairman may need to reduce his own authority.*

Don't let them wander

Many meetings lose themselves through sidetracking. Members wander off the problem-path down enticing byways and constantly need to be called back. For instance, when somebody wanders the chairman could say: 'That's an interesting point and perhaps we could deal with it later, but for the moment could we focus on . . .' You may need to allow *some* wandering time because it may lead to something relevant and usable, but too much meandering can destroy the meeting's usefulness.

If the speaker rambles on, mixing relevant with irrelevant comments, the chairman could restate the speaker's relevant points concisely then ask somebody else to go on from there: 'I think what Harry is saying is . . . Tom, do you agree with that?'

When there are many private conversations and sidetrackings the trouble may stem from the seating arrangements. When people are seated in squares or rectangles those on the corners may by squeezed out and find it difficult to become involved in the business of the meeting. This effect can be avoided by having a round-table arrangement or, if the group is large, a U-shaped arrangement. A rectangular seating arrangement with the chairman sitting at the head of the table encourages status consciousness and centralised communication patterns.

In any meeting communications tend to flow across rather than around the table (Steinzor, 1950). This has useful practical applications. For instance, you could make sure that notorious opponents were seated on the same side of the table so that they didn't monopolise the discussion.

Tell them where they are going

When you're sitting in the hot seat your primary function is to keep your attention rivetted on the road ahead. This means:

• *specifying goals* at the beginning and, if necessary, at intervals throughout the meeting
• *restating and summarising* important ideas and conclusions, thus underlining for the group the progress it is making
• *moving the discussion forward* by asking stimulating and provocative questions: not the cross-questioning type, which terrifies people into silence; but the sort that encourages people to speak from

their own experience and knowledge ('Harry, I believe you had a similar problem in the Sales Department. How did you tackle it there?')

• *remaining emotionally detached* so that you control proceedings from your head not your guts.

Often committees settle for some inferior solution because they have failed to examine enough alternatives. So when a proposal is offered, don't decide whether it's good or bad, whether to support it or reject it, but add it to your list of alternatives. Later – perhaps in future meetings – after you have had time to assess all the advantages and disadvantages, the less attractive alternatives can be eliminated.

It may by useful for the chairman to make a list of promising ideas and at the end of the meeting to read this list out and so summarise the group's thinking. If the meeting is one of a series the list provides the chairman with a permanent memory. At the start of the next meeting he will be able to say accurately what has been agreed already, so that the group don't spend the first ten or fifteen minutes catching up with themselves.

Don't drive too fast

Don't overwork the group. Allow them adequate time for dealing with complex problems. Or, if time is limited, shorten the agenda. Under time pressure, meetings often settle for some snap and inadequate solution. This only postpones trouble until later. So don't think that your meetings become more businesslike simply by cutting the time allowed. Remember Napoleon, who always lost at chess because he made his moves too fast.

Here is the agenda of a sports club meeting I once attended. Just two hours were available and the chairman had decided to cover a lot of business:

AGENDA

1. Minutes
2. Correspondence
3. Treasurer's Report
4. Secretary's Report
5. Fund-raising (how to raise £5,000)

6. Membership (how to boost it by 200)
7. Sale of land (whether to sell some land to a builder)
8. Any other business.

The chairman drove us through this lot at top speed and at the end congratulated us on a high-powered performance. We produced a bevy of ideas en route and made a lot of decisions with no time wasted. Later, it turned out they were the wrong decisions. Income and membership stayed low. And we learned we could have got a lot more for the land we sold if we'd shopped around a little first.

Of course, in the open situation of real life important matters frequently do have to be settled in a hurry, and a hasty decision may be better than a laboured assessment of all the alternatives. In my experience, a really competent chairman sticks out like a healthy thumb. Yet most people are perfectly capable of doing the job well if only they will learn the appropriate techniques then put them into practice at every opportunity. There is no substitute for experience. On the other hand, practice without theory is blind.

So first study this chapter and *learn the theory.* Then go to your meetings and *apply it.*

How do you rate as a Chairman?

1. I vary my style according to the purpose of the meeting.
2. I know how to deal with the 'hidden agenda' items — power struggles, jealousies, rivalries etc. — and so relieve the group's inner tensions.
3. I encourage people to bring their negative feelings out into the open by skilful questioning and careful listening.
4. I try not to let grown men quarrel over mere words — generalisations. When two men disagree I ask each one to *specify,* give examples of what he means.
5. Sometimes I deliberately reduce my own authority in meetings so as to create a freer atmosphere. I know three specific techniques for reducing the 'authority effect'.
6. If people wander from the problem-path I know how to call them back *with tact.*
7. I know the kind of seating arrangement which encourages interaction.

8. I help the committee to keep track of its progress by summarising the discussion from time to time and by keeping a record of promising ideas for future reference.
9. I don't overwork the committee, and give it adequate time to solve complex problems. If the time available is limited I shorten the agenda.
10. At the end of the meeting I summarise the ground covered, decisions made, any action to be taken and by whom.

3 What's the Procedure?
A Guide for Committee Secretaries

'Remember Murphy's Law, which states that if anything can possibly go wrong, it will.'

The committee secretary is the man who explains the committee's thinking throughout the organisation. He is obliged to establish relationships at all levels and so gains an understanding of how the organisation works as a whole. Thus the job is a valuable form of training for higher responsibility. More specifically, the success or failure of meetings may hinge on how skilfully the secretary does his job. If he does it well he creates the conditions for successful problem-solving.

Nothing kills creativity quicker than that awful committee procedure and jargon — the nem cons, the ex officios, the points of order. Many committees keep minutes and waste hours floundering in the stuff. Sometimes it exists as a deadening habit from the past. Always, too much of it acts on a meeting like an anaesthetic. *Yet the main aim of most committee meetings is to solve problems and make decisions, wasting as little time as possible and making full use of the talents of the participants. That is why every committee needs a secretary who cares more for ideas and people than for conventions and procedure. Ideas are more likely to spark, people are more likely to give, when procedure is simple and easy to understand.*

Even the House of Lords recognises the need for streamlining procedure from time to time – recently its proceedings have been made simpler and more businesslike. (Another welcome innovation has been the prominent placing of two clocks in the chamber as a gentle incentive to their lordships to be short-winded.) Procedures at top Government level have also been improved in recent years. Cabinet ministers, for instance, have traditionally gone into Cabinet meetings largely uninstructed on matters that didn't directly concern their own departments. But the machinery for briefing them adequately – the Think Tank – has now been established. (How many of this century's political disasters were caused by *inadequate* Cabinet briefing procedure?)

Procedure should be made to earn its keep: either it helps committee members with their work or it goes. If this test were applied to the committees on which *you* serve, how much formal procedure would remain?

My *Secretary's Handbook* offers the following tips:

· Interruptions and irrelevant remarks should be regarded as out of order.
· Any comments should be strictly relevant to the motion on the agenda sheet.
· An amendment must be proposed in accordance with the following procedure . . .
· A point of order arises when . . .

It strikes me that in the modern world this sort of stuff is as camp as a row of tents. It's ugly, it's useless – yet some people thrive on it, like collectors drooling over Victorian chamber pots. Maybe you too have been snared by its repulsive charms. *If so, make a bid for freedom and greater efficiency by drawing up new and simpler rules and asking the committee to approve them.*

'Keep strictly to the agenda' is another traditional rule. Yet often the most rewarding areas of discussion become apparent only as the meeting develops: they can't be *predicted* for inclusion on the agenda. In overformal meetings these fertile areas remain unexplored because they are not relevant to the agenda. As a committee secretary, constructive not destructive procedure should be your aim: the price is eternal vigilance and a willingness to ditch convention.

These are just some of the dangers when a committee suffers from an excess of procedure:

· influence falls to those with procedural knowhow: they may or may not have something worth saying;
· inexperienced members become snared in the meshes of the procedural net, become helpless lookers-on;
· as procedure becomes more formal, idea-production goes down;
· the creative, sensitive person shrinks into his shell, the Committee Bore flourishes. (One way to take the wind out of his cheeks is to impose a time limit on speakers: he uses his time up then shuts up.)

No committee ever had a good idea. Ideas are formed by individuals and committees can only adopt them. And one of your main duties as committee secretary is to create the conditions in which ideas flourish and to make sure that people don't feel hemmed in by overheavy procedure. How often have you stifled your own ideas in a meeting for fear of breaking one of the many rules and being rebuked by the chairman?

Constructive procedure

Yet most meetings require some procedure to work smoothly. A certain amount of structure and formal procedure will allow your committee to deal speedily and efficiently with a series of easy items (Case for/Case against/Vote is a fairly typical pattern). A structured approach is also useful for dealing with very complex matters – the allocation of resources, say, or the appraisal of capital projects. For the only hope of dealing adequately with problems of this size is to analyse the components of the problem separately and gradually see it as a whole. Synchronised thinking and systematic coverage are assured. Thus the appraisal of capital projects might best be tackled by carving the discussion into several stages:

1. Review of current projects by Project Managers
2. Estimated costs and expenses (Management Accountant)
3. Rationalisation plans (Personnel Manager)
4. Progress Reports from Site Managers
5. Committee's conclusions and recommendations.

Maier (1957) found that this kind of developmental approach led to better decisions than a 'free' unstructured approach.

Committee members themselves usually welcome a degree of formal procedure — perhaps because they feel they don't have to exert themselves to obtain a fair hearing. In my own experience, formal procedure is especially welcomed by members in the early stages of a committee's life: it enables members to bypass many of the communication problems and enables a group of people to start working together without delay.

Some meetings require a very strict procedure. This applies especially when questions of consent and representation are involved — as in an Annual General Meeting, say, or a shareholders' meeting. The procedure provides safeguards against malpractices. Again, very large meetings require strict procedure if decisions are to be hammered out of the wide range of opinions and interests represented. Thus you need to master the rules of formal assemblies so that you can apply them as necessary during meetings of this kind.[1]

In committee meetings formal procedure has the object of ensuring fair play between opposed interests and it is useful to the extent that it brings this about. Procedure should act as a catalyst, conjuring order — and solutions — out of chaos. If it fails in this then it becomes a time-wasting ritual, as undesirable as red tape or an outdated filing system.

Change or ignore your committee's procedural rules, or persuade the chairman to do so, when they are slowing down the proceedings, causing frustration or inhibiting the discussion. Be sensitive to people's preferences: some people prefer a structured, analytical approach; others prefer more tentative and 'wide open' methods. In any case remember that as members get to know each other they develop a group-approach to problems and there is an increasing preference for UNWRITTEN procedures.

Brief yourself

For a committee *chairman* lack of background information about items on the agenda is no disqualifier provided he has an agile mind and

---

[1] Most of the procedure used in meetings is based on the rules that govern debates in the House of Commons. T. Erskine May's *Parliamentary Practice* (18th edn., rev. B. Cocks, Butterworth, 1971) and R. F. D. Palgrave's *Chairman's Handbook* (rev. G. F. M. Campion and L. A. Abraham, Deur, 1964) are the authoritative works on the subject.

knows how to handle people. But for a committee *secretary* such innocence can be disastrous because he is the one man members rely on for background knowledge and supporting information. Members rely on the secretary for advice about such matters as which items the committee should deal with and which should be fed into the regular administrative machine; which of the alternative proposals are practical in legal and financial terms; which alternatives are preferred by other parts of the organisation. Thus the secretary needs to brief himself very thoroughly so that he can adequately brief others on the committee.

Here are some other reasons why the secretary needs to take his job very seriously:

· He is the committee's memory and therefore its guide;
· He is an essential link-man — the one man members can contact between meetings;
· He is the man responsible for explaining the committee's thinking throughout the organisation. This obliges him to establish working relationships at all levels and gives him the chance to gain an overall understanding of what goes on in the organisation. Thus acting as a committee secretary can be a valuable form of training for general management.

To fulfil all these functions well he needs to establish easy relationships with all the members of the committee — how else could he get to know the committee's 'thinking' at any given time? Thus he cannot afford to take sides, in or out of meetings. Otherwise he loses authority with the group as a whole and sacrifices its trust, and his usefulness to the committee drops.

As committee secretary you occupy a pivotal position for the success or failure of meetings can hinge on how skilfully you tackle your secretarial chores. Acting as a kind of choreographer you train the members to improve their routines, and feed them with the advice and information they need to work together creatively. For instance, at the beginning of each meeting you may brief members on the history of the subject under discussion, provide them with the broad alternatives together with information about costs, practical target dates, legal considerations, and so on. This kind of servicing creates the conditions for successful problem-solving.

Even a clumsy and inexperienced committee can add polish to its performance if guided, advised and briefed by a skilled secretary.

31

The before-and-after chores

A. BEFORE THE MEETING: You can't prepare for an important meeting too thoroughly. Remember Murphy's Law which states that if anything can possibly go wrong it will.

1. Prepare *yourself* for the meeting by thoroughly briefing yourself on all agenda items.
2. Draw up and circulate the convening notice.
3. Draw up and circulate the agenda in consultation with the chairman.
4. Assemble background information and include this in working papers. Circulate these at least forty-eight hours before the meeting.
5. Make a list of any files, record books, correspondence etc. that you will need to take to the meeting, including any records you may need to refer to in case awkward questions are asked. (Like a Cabiner Minister at Question Time you never know what the supplementary questions will bring.)
6. Approach any manager or official who should be present at the meeting to answer questions, present reports etc. Confirm their agreement to attend by memo.
7. Check that the room will be free and that caretakers, technicians etc. will be on duty at the right time. Arrange for blackboards, visual aids and other equipment which may be required to be available.

FACTORY SAFETY COMMITTEE

A meeting will be held on 4th January 1974.

Please will you inform the secretary if you

are unable to attend.

_____ Secretary

Fig. 8: Notice of a committee meeting.

THE SOCIETY OF CIVIL ENGINEERING TECHNICIANS

1-7 GREAT GEORGE STREET-WESTMINSTER-LONDON-SW1

TELEPHONE: 01-839 3611   TELEGRAMS: INSTITUTION, LONDON, SW1

NOTICE

NOTICE IS HEREBY GIVEN THAT THE

ANNUAL GENERAL MEETING

of the
SOCIETY OF CIVIL ENGINEERING TECHNICIANS
will be held on
FRIDAY 10th OCTOBER 1973
at the
INSTITUTION OF CIVIL ENGINEERS
1-7 Great George St.
London, S.W.1
at
6.0.p.m.

Fig. 9:   Notice of an Annual General Meeting.

B. AFTER THE MEETING

1. Draw up the minutes or the report of the meeting and circulate to interested parties.
2. Communicate the committee's decisions to any interested parties.
3. Check with people who have been asked to take action that they are clear about what is required, timing, budgets etc. Give additional briefing if necessary.
4. Take any follow-up actions which are necessary, such as telephone calls, letters, requisitions, invitations to tender, bookings etc.

All these chores can make your duties almost as demanding as a full-time job. Preparing working papers for the committee, for instance, can take up a great deal of time. But this particular chore is a vital one for decisions become much sharper, much more on-target, when all the facts are on the table. Working papers are especially helpful when the information they contain is related to the members themselves and show what individuals or departments will gain or lose by particular proposals.

THE SOCIETY OF CIVIL ENGINEERING
TECHNICIANS

1-7 GREAT GEORGE STREET-WESTMINSTER-LONDON-SW1

TELEPHONE: 01-839 3611   TELEGRAMS: INSTITUTION, LONDON, S.W.1.

AGENDA

1. To receive the notice convening the meeting
2. To approve the Minutes of the Inaugural Meeting held on the 27th June 1972
3. To receive the Annual Report of the Society
4. To receive the Balance Sheet and Statement of Accounts for the financial year ending 30th June 1973
5. To approve the election of members of the Executive Committee
6. To authorise the appointment and payment of Auditors for the financial year ending 30th. June 1974

Fig. 10:   An agenda sheet for an Annual General Meeting. *The agenda for a committee meeting is usually drawn up by the Secretary in consultation with the Chairman.*

But don't *over*-inform members. If they feel they have *all* the information they need to reach a decision before the meeting starts they may take up firm positions and use the meeting to defend them and convert others. If the problem had been as simple as that there would have been no need for a meeting in the first place.

The secretary is the group's memory

The secretary's most important function is to act as the group's memory and therefore its guide. He fixes this memory in writing (occasionally on tape), varying the format to suit the needs of the committee and the organisation. With the help of this record he makes sure that past, present and future decisions interlock and so helps the group to move forward in a straight line.

People have extremely unreliable memories. They recall imperfectly what was said and done only days before. (Exactly what was said in the last meeting *you* attended?) Relying on people's memories is unsound management, especially when important issues are at stake. This applies to all aspects of business life, including committee meetings.

The secretary's notebook is a vital memory aid. Into it goes the raw material from which he shapes the committee's official records. This raw material may include:

- statements of problems discussed
- suggested solutions
- other promising ideas
- all formal motions, precisely and in full
- names of proposers and seconders
- votes for and against
- names of members attending
- details of actions recommended by the committee

Not all this information will be used in the official minutes or report. The secretary's notebook is usually as chaotic and all-inclusive as the final record is ordered and selective. Everything goes into the notebook because it will be used not only for writing up the minutes but also to settle any future dispute about what was said and when, who said it, what the plan was, what the alternatives were, and so on. It also reminds the secretary to take follow-up actions after meetings.

Encourage members to state their ideas clearly for you may need to act on them. If a motion is vaguely worded, say so, or better still suggest a better way of expressing it. Otherwise, next week, when the minutes are read out, the committee may not be sure what it had in mind.

If two or three separate motions express basically the same idea you could save yourself unnecessary labour, and help the committee to get its thinking focused, by suggesting a single composite motion: 'Mr Chairman, I wonder if a motion on the following lines would satisfy all three proposers . . .'

Not every meeting, though, requires a formal record It would be pointless, for instance, to keep a record of a gripe-session where the objective is merely to give people the opportunity to express their feelings.

What *kind* of record should you compose from your notebook? In one Midlands engineering firm all committees have formal *minutes* which are kept in the Personnel office where anybody may consult them at any time; but they also send short *reports* of meetings, highlighting interesting ideas, to the board and department heads. In another firm, subcommittees send formal *minutes* of their proceedings to the parent committees, by whom they are 'received'. But they also post *memos* on all notice boards listing all recommendations made.

Writing the minutes

The motion is the pivot of formal committee meetings. Discussion on an item begins when a motion is proposed and seconded. It ends when a vote is taken and the motion is either thrown out or accepted, when it becomes a resolution. Formal meetings exist, as it were, to pass resolutions.

For meetings like this minutes are the best form of record. Apart from preserving the usual routine information (numbers present, time the meeting opened etc.) minutes consist of a record of resolutions passed. Thus they summarise the business done at the meeting. Figure 11 shows typical minutes of a formal committee meeting.

Minutes are easy to write when members can be persuaded to put their motions in writing and, after moving them, to pass them to the secretary. This practice ensures a completely accurate minute. More important, it encourages proposers to think first about exactly what they want to propose before speaking.

Make sure that each resolution begins with the word That, and record it as simply as possible. Why not, for instance, simply use the word Resolved to introduce each minute? This practice makes minutes easier to write, easier to refer back to. Personal references to proposers and seconders are unnecessary because resolutions are binding on the whole committee (the only way to escape responsibility for a resolution is to resign from the committee). Try to make sure that resolutions are worded *concisely and in the affirmative* – they are much clearer that way.

VAGUE, WORDY, NEGATIVE	CONCISE AND POSITIVE
	Machinery: lunch-time arrangement
1. It was proposed by Mr E. Smith, seconded by Mr A. Bennett, that no machinery should be switched off during the period 1.30 to 2.15 daily	RESOLVED: That machines should be left ON during the lunch hour.

Bank Account

2. Proposed by Mr A. Harmer, seconded by Mr R. Edwards, that a Current Account be opened with the National Westminster Bank and that no fewer than two directors' signatures should be required as authorisation for that Bank for the payment of moneys.

RESOLVED: That a current Account be opened with the National Westminster Bank and that signatures of two directors shall be required on cheques.

Photocopier

3. RESOLVED: that the company shall not at this time purchase a new photocopier and that rather than approach a supplier, advertisements should be placed in the local Press for the purchase of a secondhand machine.

RESOLVED: That we should advertise locally for a secondhand copier.

Write up the minutes from your notebook soon after the meeting. Give each separate minute its own heading to help your reader to find what he wants fast. Try to get the minutes duplicated and circulated within forty-eight hours, while the events of the meeting are still fresh in people's minds. Remember that there is no legal obligation to read the minutes aloud at the next meeting for members to approve, though this is a common ritual. Under the Companies Act 1948, all they require to be made valid is the chairman's signature — at the bottom of each page if they are typed or printed.

When NOT to write minutes

The trouble with minutes is that the really interesting, creative ideas that emerge in a meeting may never get recorded. If this is happening with your meetings, why not write reports instead of minutes? Reports are more appropriate than minutes when:

(*a*) the meeting is exploratory, informal, free-flowing;

Education Committee, 18th October 1971 (continued).

Estimates of Capital Expenditure, 1972/73.

★5. The City Education Officer has presented to us estimates of
capital expenditure showing in detail under the various
heads the estimated total costs of approved projects, actual
expenditure to 31st March 1971, estimated expenditure for
the current financial year and for the year 1972/73 and after
(*a copy of the report having been sent previously to each
member*).

We *Recommend*: That the estimates of capital expenditure
as presented to us for the period 1972/73, totalling
£1,629,270 made up as follows, be approved for submission
to the County Council:-

Nursery Schools	£7,950
Primary Schools	£597,560
Secondary Schools	£922,030
Special Schools	£3,300
Provision of Milk, Meals and other Refreshments	£98,430
Facilities for Recreation and Social and Physical Training	—
	£1,629,270

Capital Programme, 1972/77.

6. We have received and considered a detailed report showing
the implications of our capital programme as envisaged for
the five year period 1972/77 (*a copy of the report having been
sent previously to each member*). The report covers projects
now under construction and those approved by the Department of Education and Science for the Starts List 1972/73
and the Design List 1972/73, together with a forecast of
items which we might reasonably expect to be included in
programmes during the period under review.

We have accepted the report as submitted to us for inclusion
in the comprehensive assessment of all services to be
prepared by the City Treasurer, as follows:-

1972/73	£1,688,770	1975/76	£890,870
1973/74	£1,176,900	1976/77	£962,050
1974/75	£833,640		

Fig. 11: Extract from the minutes of an Education Committee meeting.

(*b*) ideas and arguments are more important than any definite decisions.

Thus for most problem-solving meetings a report would be more useful than minutes, because in that kind of meeting asides, interjections and casual remarks usually give as many useful leads as any number of formal proposals. Yet these valuable throwaway contributions would never get recorded in formal minutes.

When writing a report of a meeting aim at giving a clear understanding of collective thinking, highlighting any agreements or conclusions reached. Or, if *disagreement* was the crux of the meeting, express this in focused form so that people can see the extent of the differences at a glance, as it were:

> During the meeting held on 1 September 1973 three alternative proposals for improving recruitment policy were suggested:
> (*a*) employing consultants
> (*b*) use of personality tests
> (*c*) making heads of department responsible for personnel selection.

Then fill in the details.

By summarising the entire report in the opening paragraph you save people the bother of wading through the whole document just to get some idea of what the meeting accomplished.

Organising a brainstorming session

To hold a brainstorming session all you need is a tape-recorder, a relaxed atmosphere and between ten and twenty people, preferably from different disciplines.

The idea of a brainstorming session is to generate as many ideas as possible on a given topic ('How to raise £1 million') in a given time. Nobody is allowed to criticise anybody else's ideas, no matter how ridiculous they may seem. Participants are encouraged really to let themselves go. All ideas are welcome – practical and impractical alike – because the emphasis at this stage is on quantity not quality; and sometimes an impractical idea becomes completely practical if slightly modified.

So no criticisms, no rejections, no judgments. Analysis and quality control will follow – but only after the meeting has ended. So it all becomes an exciting game. Enthusiasm and the idea count soar,

Voting: the pros and cons

Advantages	Disadvantages
1 Voting is essential where questions of consent are involved — e.g. the election of directors at a shareholders' meeting.	1 Factions or departmental cliques may form. Members tend to see themselves as Us (likely to vote For) and Them (likely to vote Against). Instead of tackling problems together, opposing sides spend much time and energy fighting each other.
2 Voting is useful when it would be difficult to reach a decision otherwise as, for example, in some interdepartmental meetings or in Parliament.	2 Voting makes issues appear black and white rather than in their true grey tones so that lop-sided decisions may be made.
3 Voting is a quick and convenient way of testing how members feel about a particular issue. In the case of company committees the results of voting can provide management with valuable feedback.	3 Idea-production may suffer as a result of members censoring ideas which they believe the majority will vote against.
4 Voting can end prolonged conflict and resolve crises, in the same way that a General Election does.	4 There is a danger of wheeling-dealing and of spheres of influence being agreed. For instance, school governorships are sometimes apportioned on the basis of 'You vote for our man and we'll vote for yours'.
	5 As the experience of some trade unions shows, small determined groups can develop tactics for winning votes and manipulating decisions.

Fig. 12:

provided that the organiser has successfully created a free and uninhibited atmosphere.[1]

Later, the taped discussion is transcribed in the form of a verbatim report which is carefully scrutinised for possible leads. The most promising ideas are selected and developed.

[1] Though Taylor *et al.*, 1958, found that a number of individuals working *alone* throw up more ideas than the same number working as a group.

The secretary's role during meetings

Problems	Suggested solutions (see below)
*Inexperienced chairman with little control of proceedings.	2 3 6 7
*Meetings flounder; members ramble; little progress is made.	1 2 5 6
*There are many opinions, few facts and no sustained arguments.	3 8
*Vaguely-worded motions are passed. Sometimes members are unclear about exactly what has been decided or what administrative action will be required.	8
*Parkinson's Law of Triviality operates: time spent on any item is inversely proportional to its importance. £500,000 may be voted for a building project after ten minutes' brisk opinion-giving. But the committee may take an hour deciding where to place a new coffee machine.	6 7
*Evaluation of proposals is weak or non-existent, so that poor-quality or irrational decisions are sometimes made.	4 8 9
*Procedure is either too heavy or too light.	2

Solutions

1 If the discussion is one of a series on the same problem briefly summarise the work accomplished in previous sessions at the beginning of the meeting. This will help the members to get their ideas straight and remind them of the issues which remain to be covered. If it is decided to hold another meeting on the same problem you could indicate the amount of unfinished work in the notice of the next meeting.

2 Discuss procedure with the chairman before the meeting begins and provide him with guidelines, e.g. if complex matters have to be dealt with you might suggest that the discussion should be broken into stages so that members can deal systematically with one aspect at a time.

3 Brief the chairman before the meeting. Provide him with background information about items which will be discussed, what company policy is, what various members think, and so on. Thus he will be able to conduct the meeting with his eyes open and he will also be able to give members enough background information for them to discuss items intelligently.

4 If it looks to you that the decision that is about to be taken is the wrong one and springs from incomprehension or misinformation, why not find some reason for delaying the decision? — such as some new facts which need probing, some questions which need answering, somebody who needs to be consulted. A delay will give members time to think again and give you more time to produce further information.

5 Suggest to the chairman that the discussion might be continued at a later meeting because agreement is unlikely at this one . . . Alternatively, remind the members through the chairman that a decision **is** needed even if it is on one which doesn't meet all requirements.

6 Unobtrusively take over some of the chairman's functions — e.g. by tactfully summarising from time to time so as to give a sense of direction or to put an end to pointless discussion: 'I'd like to get my own ideas clear: are we saying that . . .'

7 When a good idea emerges keep the committee's attention focused on it: 'Could you explain how that method would work out here?' Thus the speaker is encouraged to develop and improve his point and a valuable idea is given prominence.

8 Counter **opinion**-giving by feeding the committee with **facts, figures and information.** Watch out for important points that have been overlooked then remind members of them: 'Mr Chairman, I think we should remember that there is less than £5000 left in this fund and this greatly restricts our freedom of action.'

9 Ask members to put motions in writing. This encourages them to get their own thoughts into focus and makes minute-writing easier and surer. Propositions are often vague because they try to say too much. When this happens a useful remedial action is to split the motion into two or more parts and take separate votes on each. On the other hand, you may wish to speed up proceedings by inviting the proposers of two or three very similar motions to combine them into a single composite motion. At the end of the meeting make a point of agreeing with members on any administrative actions that need to be taken before the next meeting.

Fig. 13:

Organising a problem-solving meeting

There are many ways of solving problems and making decisions. There are dictatorial decisions, decisions by majority rule, decisions by minority rule, decisions by unanimous consent, and so on. Sometimes a technical expert solving problems alone gets good results: this applies especially when the problem is the kind that has a 'correct' answer (e.g. a costing or pricing problem) and where a 'democratic' decision could easily lose the company thousands of pounds.

At other times the group approach to problem-solving is more effective. For instance, when the participants' acceptance of a decision is important (e.g. devising new overtime schedules); or when a pooling of ideas is likely to add to the quality of the decision (e.g. ways of improving safety procedures).

Group problem-solving techniques require careful study and the training of key individuals, such as the committee secretary, who can then train other members in the method.[1] Once mastered, problem-solving method can be applied at all levels in the organisation. For instance, brickyard foremen in Peterborough learnt some of the techniques, then held problem-solving meetings with their own sections. The solutions reached were accepted by management and successfully implemented.

The techniques

People in a meeting often come up with an answer before they have explored the problem. The result is poor quality decisions, for the answer to any problem is no better than our formulation of it. To stop this happening why not advise the chairman to split the discussion into three stages: (*a*) discussing the problem, (*b*) suggesting solutions, and (*c*) evaluating solutions and making a decision. This approach will ensure that the committee will at least circle round a problem before thundering in with a solution.

Stage A: Discussing the Problem
The chairman or secretary begins by stating the problem in detail and as *factually* as possible: 'The problem is to find ways of reducing typing costs. O and M feel that the cost of producing letters in this company is far too high – they've come up with the figure of £1 per letter. Some of the background facts are in the working paper which you have in front of you. As you can see, we employ 36 typists at a total annual cost of £31,000. In addition, there are certain overheads . . .'

Facts and figures follow. Important factors are emphasised – total output, supervision arrangements, comparisons with other firms etc. At this stage the group is invited to contribute with specific instances and observations, making the problem into a kind of case study. People with ideas for *solving* the problems are told to hold their horses until Stage 2 of the proceedings. Discussion of the problem is not allowed to go on so long that members become buried in detail and analysis, only long enough to acquaint them with the main facts.

[1] An essential first step is to read Norman Maier's book, *Problem-solving Discussions and Conferences*, McGraw-Hill, 1963.

Stage B: Suggesting Solutions

By now members will have a good grasp of the problem and, provided the atmosphere is informal and relaxed, ideas for solving it will be bubbling.[1] Your job as secretary is to catch these ideas as they burst and record them for future evaluation.

As in a brainstorming session, only criticisms and negative comments like 'That won't work' are forbidden. Silly and apparently irrelevant remarks are tolerated because they may contain the seeds of a solution (in the creative process the irrational component is more important than the intellectual). And so in a friendly permissive atmosphere members cross-fertilise each other's suggestions and, almost by a process of free association, solutions begin to emerge. As J. J. Gordon has pointed out in *Synectics*, a 'free-wheeling' group can compress into a few hours the kind of semiconscious mental activity which might take months of incubation for a single person – depending on the willingness of members to take psychological chances and abandon familiar ways of looking at things.

Remember that most problems permit of several solutions and that if the search ends too soon the optimum solution may never be born. Maier and Hoffman, 1960, found that group solutions were of higher quality when test groups were instructed to find a second solution after they thought they had already solved the problem.

Stage C: Evaluating Solutions and Making a Decision

Begin this stage of the discussion by reminding the group of the alternative choices that have emerged. Next, make sure the group evaluates each possible solution by using Norman Maier's two-column method. Two columns are chalked on the board, headed respectively 'Advantages' and 'Disadvantages'. Each alternative is then evaluated with points being entered in the appropriate columns. (As well as isolating the disadvantages, the group should think about ways in which they could be overcome.) Thus a complex situation is broken down and a balanced evaluation of each alternative is assured.

The alternatives are then rated in order of preference and the discussion focuses on how to keep the advantages of the most favoured

[1] Under certain conditions a tight, authoritarian structure can help with creative problem-solving – e.g. in a critical or competitive environment as when, in an advertising agency, two teams are asked to produce rival campaigns.

solution and how to get round the disadvantages. Finally the group decides on what action is needed to implement the decision.

The short and easy way of decision-making is by majority vote, but this method causes committees to split into rival camps and individuals to plump for all-or-nothing choices. Minds clamp shut. Grey disappears. True evaluation stops.

The approach to problem-solving outlined above follows the ideas of Norman Maier, Franklyn Haiman, Irving Lee and George Prince. It has many practical implications in business. Any committee wishing to experiment with the method would first have to make suitable training arrangements for its chairman and secretary.

What do you know about committee procedure?

The answers are on page 47.

Questions	Answer

1   A British court has ruled that, to be valid, a motion requires
    a) one seconder
    b) two seconders
    c) no seconders

2   A committee member raises a Point of Order if he is dissatisfied
    with
    a) the way the chairman answers a question
    b) the conduct of members — e.g. bad language
    c) the regularity or otherwise of proceedings — e.g.
       infringements of the constitution

3   When a Point of Order is raised,
    a) the committee itself decides the issue by voting
    b) following a short general discussion, the secretary gives
       a decision
    c) no discussion or vote is allowed — the chairman's decision
       is final

4   In formal committee meetings
    a) discussion of an item on the agenda **begins** with a motion
       being proposed
    b) discussion on an item **ends** with a motion being proposed
       and immediately voted on
    c) all motions to be proposed during the meeting are read
       aloud by the secretary as soon as the meeting opens

5 A resolution is
    a) another word for a motion
    b) a motion that has been voted on and accepted
    c) a recommendation by a sub-committee to a parent
       committee

6 Most of the rules governing the conduct of official company
committees are laid down
    a) in the Companies Act, 1948
    b) in the company's Articles of Association
    c) by the Managing Director or Chairman of the company

7 Standing Orders are
    a) written rules, governing the conduct and procedure of
       committee meetings
    b) written company policy regarding membership and
       responsibilities of committees
    c) the record of a company committee's decisions once
       they've been approved by the board

8 A quorum is
    a) the minimum number of members that a committee
       must have
    b) the smallest number of members who must be present
       for the proceedings of a meeting to be valid
    c) the number of members who need to be present
       before an AGM can start

9 What constitutes a quorum is stated by
    a) the Secretary of the committee
    b) the Chairman of the committee
    c) the committee's Standing Orders

10 The objective of having a quorum is
    a) that the meeting should be truly representative of
       the membership
    b) to discourage hole-and-corner methods
    c) to ensure lively meetings

11 To suspend Standing Orders — e.g. so that a meeting may
continue beyond the normal time — a $\frac{2}{3}$ vote is usually
required.
       TRUE   or   FALSE

12 An Amendment to a motion usually involves the addition,
omission or alteration of a single word or several words in
the original motion.
       TRUE   or   FALSE

13 Once an Amendment to a motion has been approved, the
motion as amended need not be voted on but is automatically
accepted.

TRUE   or   FALSE

14 Adjourned **sine die** means

15 Elected **ex officio** means

16 Carried **nem. con.** means

What's the procedure — answers

1 — c

2 — b or c

3 — c

4 — a

5 — b

6 — b

7 — a But many organisations never
draw up Standing Orders — e.g.
many Trade Unions — and
rely instead on unwritten
rules and conventions.

8 — b

9 — c

10 — a or b

11 — TRUE

12 — TRUE. An amendment objects
to **details** only and is not valid
if, in effect, it entirely rejects
the motion.

13 — FALSE. Sometimes the
amendment is approved —
perhaps as the lesser of two evils
— but the **motion as amended**
is rejected.

14 — Adjourned **without a fixed date**
for meeting again.

15 — Elected **by virtue of his office.**

16 — Carried **without anybody
opposing** (though some may
have abstained).

Fig. 14:

Reminders

1. As a committee secretary you are an essential link man. You are
   the man who explains the committee's thinking throughout the
   organisation. This makes the job an excellent form of training for
   higher responsibility.

2. Too much formality and procedure kill creativity and give
   influence to those with procedural know-how: would new and
   simpler procedural rules help *your* committee to streamline its
   performance?

3. Have you mastered the rules of formal assemblies so that you can apply them when necessary? – e.g. in very large meetings, or in meetings where questions of consent and representation make formal procedures necessary (for instance, local government committees).

4. The secretary's responsibilities include
   - preparing the notice, agenda and working papers of meetings
   - making physical preparations for the meeting
   - contacting any officials or managers who should be present to answer questions etc.
   - communicating the committee's decisions to interested parties
   - taking necessary follow-up actions after meetings
   - drawing up minutes or reports of proceedings and circulating them

5. Your notebook is a vital piece of equipment. Into it goes all the information needed
   - to write the minutes or report of the meeting
   - to settle any later disputes about what was said or agreed
   - to take any necessary follow-up actions after meetings

6. Minutes are the best form of record for formal meetings which pivot around formal motions. Reports are more suitable for informal meetings where ideas and arguments are more important than any formal motions.

7. Resolutions should be recorded in the minutes concisely and in the affirmative ('RESOLVED: That machinery should be left ON in the lunch hour').

8. When writing the report of a meeting, summarise what was accomplished in the opening paragraph to save busy executives having to plough through the entire document to find out.

9. An effective problem-solving method is to split the session into three distinct stages: (*a*) discussing the problem, (*b*) suggesting solutions, and (*c*) evaluating solutions and making a decision.

10. Problem-solving method needs careful study and the training of the secretary and chairman before it can be applied, though once mastered it can be used at all levels in the organisation.

4 Influencing Committees
A guide for people who attend meetings

'. . . the hermit-drab who never steps into the light to blow the dust off his ideas'

For the young manager on the way up, one of the best vehicles is the committee meeting: it presents him with the opportunity to influence the decision-makers and to make his talents available to the entire organisation. One drawback is that all committees develop a definite pecking-order in terms of the amount of influence permitted, and the newcomer is likely to find himself at the back of the queue. How can an inexperienced committeeman set about increasing his status and influence in meetings? This chapter suggests some ways and means.

The more complex a company becomes the more it relies on teamwork and coordination. Different experts handle different aspects of problems which are themselves only components of larger problems. Each job is a communication exercise on a grand scale.[1]

In this kind of environment the poor communicator gets damaged. The walled-in specialist, the hermit-drab who never steps into the light to blow the dust off his ideas for inspection and approval, repeatedly sees inferior but crisply presented plans accepted in preference to his own. Good communicators are usually better rewarded. These are the men who are able and willing to exhibit their ideas, and their communication skills, in the presence of their enemies and friends. Thus they are well placed to improve their status and influence in the company. In particular, attending company meetings presents the specialist and the junior manager with golden opportunities to make his talents available to the whole organisation. Here is his chance to influence the decision-makers and to draw the attention of the top men to his high-flying executive qualities. William Whyte has, somewhat satirically, drawn attention to the 'conference way' of self-improvement:

> For a young man on the make there is no better vehicle than the conference way . . . via the conference he can expose himself to all sorts of superiors across the line of command. Given minimum committeemanship skills, by an adroit question here and a modest suggestion there, he can call attention to himself and still play the game.[2]

Like it or not, you have to work on and through committees to achieve your goals. And you can operate more effectively if you know some of the characteristics of committees and the dynamics which are involved.

Ask yourself these questions

Imagine that you have been invited to sit on the company's Production Committee. You want to make an effective contribution but how can

---

[1] In *The Management of Innovation*, Burns and Stalker have reported the effect of organisational structure on electronics firms. In the rapidly changing environment of the electronics industry firms with 'organic' structure survived, those with 'mechanistic' structure failed. In an organic organisation direct contact between individuals at differing levels and free interaction between different specialists is allowed for. Lines of communication are not rigidly structured.

[2] William Whyte, *The Organisation Man* (Simon and Schuster, 1956) p. 152.

you make sure that this happens? What can you do to prepare yourself? Begin by asking yourself these questions:

· Have you been brought in to fill a gap: are you replacing the only accountant or the only Personnel man on the committee? If so, your role has been largely defined for you.

· Will you be expected to represent a department, section, group of specialists, or some other special interest?

· Have you been brought in to beef up the committee's competence in a particular area? If so, you will know in which directions to make your most strenuous efforts.

· Are you expected to play the same role as your predecessor on the committee — for instance, the Bright Young Man full of radical ideas; or the Marketing whizz-kid; or the sound no-nonsense executive?

The answer to these questions will show you the kind of contribution you're *expected* to make. It's your choice whether to live up to or disappoint these expectations.

Study your committee colleagues

1. *Get to know the personal and group characteristics of your committee colleagues as soon as possible. Once you know the sort of people they are you'll be able to take the approaches and plan the kinds of campaign which, with this particular group, will get the best results. Find out what you can about them. Study them during meetings: their likes and dislikes, their strong and weak points, the way they speak, the way they react to different ideas. If this sounds a bit hard and unfeeling remember that THEY are scrutinising YOU just as keenly.*

You'll want to know each man's position in the company's hierarchy; who the unofficial leaders are; what their various specialisms are. (Unless you enjoy being broken, don't cross anybody of marked authority at this early stage.) Is anyone likely to take a particular line on any particular issue? Is the committee as a whole cautious or radical in approach? What kind of proposals will it and won't it accept?

You need to collect this information systematically so that you don't ride into battle unarmed.

2. *Find out which members are, secretly or openly, committed to representing special interests, such as a trade union, a particular department or a clique or employees.* This knowledge will tell you which people and which topics need to be approached with special care.

3. *Identify the bigot as soon as possible so that you can devise tactics for dealing with him.* The bigot sees the world through the focus of his own prejudices. He comes to the meeting with a closed mind and with the problem already fully solved in his own mind. You can't argue with him and he won't accept compromise. Sometimes the only tactic is to ensure that he forms a minority of one.

Learn as much about your committee colleagues as possible so that you will neither underestimate nor overestimate them – both dangerous mistakes. Knowing their strengths and weaknesses you will be able to adopt the most effective tactics for dealing with them, and to determine which topics and which people need treating with special caution.

Winning status

Groups develop a definite pecking order in terms of the amount of speech and influence permitted. A person's place in the queue is mainly a function of how useful he has been to the group in the past. Thus, as a newcomer to any committee your status is bound to be low – although I know of one man, an MP, who was co-opted on to the committee of a cricket club and, during his first meeting, persuaded the other members to change the club rules and alter the fixture list. But unless you can claim membership of the House of Commons or some other high-ranking group, *your* climb to influence is bound to be slower.

Persons of high rank feel free to interrupt people of lower status in the group. But if you are a low-ranking member little notice will be taken of what you say. By a subtle system of rewards and punishments the group will keep you in your place, make you keep a civil tongue, even – in the long run – make you think the way they do.[1] *In time, the members of a committee come to resemble one another in their behaviour and thinking by incorporating group norms into their own private ones. Hence the common experience of members of joint*

---

[1] Majority pressure can be almost irresistible. In one famous experiment each of 123 subjects was asked, in turn, to say which of three lines was the same length as another line after five stooges had all given a wrong judgment: 37 per cent of the subjects were wrong whereas normally the error is less than 1 per cent. S. E. Asch studied college students' assessments of various professions: most subjects raised their own valuation of the profession of politics after being told that the other students had judged politics highest with regard to intelligence, social usefulness etc.

consultative, local government, interdepartmental and other kinds of committee – including the House of Commons – drifting away from the people they are supposed to be representing.

New members of a committee have low status, and low-status participants typically confine their contributions to requests for information and opinions and expressions of agreement or disagreement. So clearly, to make any sort of impact on your new committee you need to win status fast, though once you've won it there will be new problems waiting. One of these problems is that the high-ranking member feels a strong pressure to conform (his position depends on it). This can reduce his usefulness to the organisation by tempting him to pull his punches, connive at misguided policies, and so on. As an established committee man it is not easy to maintain an independent judgment and critical alertness. Yet these are the very qualities you can exercise without strain or fear during your first months on the committee. You'll be free to express your ideas but you won't get them accepted: for this you need status: the only way to beat the system is to appear to join it.

Speeding your climb

Through the decades, loyal selfless service alone will carry you up the committee pyramid and gild you with influence. But if you can't wait that long the following tactics should speed your upward climb:

1. Make sure that when your committee colleagues first size you up you are couth, kempt and shevelled with the Mr Hyde in you carefully cloaked. When people meet for the first time the first half-hour is spent in weighing each other up and only after this game has ended do they start to listen to each other.[1] *In the crucial early stages of your membership members are judging how much faith they can put in your ideas from your appearance and manner.* As Antony Jay has commented: 'Most narrow decisions, I am convinced, come down more often than anyone yet accepts to primitive tribal acclamation, to a man or a small group of men winning the confidence and respect of another

---

[1] Experiments by Maslow with apes and Lorenz with dogs show that a sizing-up process goes on when animals meet, subsequently developing into a dominant-submissive relationship. How much of the human sizing-up process goes on below the level of consciousness – unconscious responses to voice, manner etc.?

group.'[1] Whether you will be granted entry into this select and influential band can depend on such trivia as hair-style, the way you dress, and party manners.

2. *In early meetings, simply talking wins you prestige and a reputation for productivity.* The Laboratory of Social Relations has been studying groups and meetings for nearly thirty years. Surprisingly, it concludes that talkative members usually contribute the most helpful remarks and have the best ideas and that other members recognise this.

If your fellow-members judge you productive in early meetings they will expect you to be productive in future meetings too: this expectation will, by reflection, increase your confidence at a time when you need it most.

The price to be paid is that if you continue being talkative in meeting after meeting, you lose friends and influence people: you are likely to become influential but also unpopular, perhaps because productivity is felt as a kind of control and so resented.

3. *Participate early and make your presence felt throughout the meeting.* As soon as the meeting starts deliberately break away from your self-centred thoughts, deliberately focus on the problem facing the committee, and contribute. The earlier you do this the greater your total contribution is likely to be, and this will underpin your reputation for productivity. Sometimes, though, it is better to reserve your contribution for later in the discussion: for instance, if the committee is discussing a very controversial matter it may be a good idea to make your own speech immediately before the vote so that there are no hard-hitting replies.

4. *The amount of preparation you do will largely determine whether the other members judge you an acquisition or a bore; whether they ignore you or listen to what you say with respect.* Unless quality of presentation matches quality of ideas *your* proposal may be the one that got away. Preparation and adequate self-briefing compensate for inexperience whereas a blank mind leaves its logotype on all your contributions.

When all the members arrive at a meeting unprepared and inadequately briefed decisions tend to be made by High Speed Guess. This frequently happens on town council committees, and incidentally raises the question of whether laymen are the right people to take decisions

---

[1] A. Jay, *Effective Presentation: communication of ideas by words and visual aids*, Management Publications, 1971, p. 65.

on such complex matters as town planning, educational arrangements and local taxation.

So prepare yourself for meetings by following these guidelines:

· Carefully read all working papers circulated in advance;

· Study the agenda: decide which items are, for you, the important ones: these will be the ones where you will make your major contributions. Brief yourself thoroughly on these topics so that you don't waste the meeting's time asking questions you could have answered for yourself.

· Prepare any written or visual aids that you wish to use in the meeting to add impact to your contribution – handouts, charts, flip-boards and the like.

· If you are an inexperienced speaker, why not write out in full all the points you plan to make? Boil down this script into brief notes which you can take into the meeting and use as a speaking aid. Practise speaking from those notes. In the meeting the right phrasing will come to you as you go along and you will find it easy to expand each brief reference to almost any length you like.

Notes arranged under headings and subheadings are very easy to follow in the bustle of a lively meeting – here are some which I found very helpful on one occasion:

1. *Create local interest*

A. *Press*
 ads
 letters
 see editors
 Press conf.
 stunts?

B. *TV*
 Ring Ian
 agencies

2. *Cut down expenses*

A. *Overdraft*
 new building
 sell equipment
 salaries

B. *Higher subs.*
 Area
 Region

Overpreparation has its dangers. It can make you misjudge a complex issue so that you arrive at the meeting knowing all the answers. And too much input can create an overload effect. In one experiment members of discussion groups were given either two, four or six possible solutions to a human relations problem. Usually the member with only two solutions dominated his group both in quantity and quality of contributions.

By adopting the four general approaches outlined above you should be able to raise your status in the group and create the conditions for influencing its thinking.

Riding the emotional waves

Conflict in meetings is not always destructive. People do not always see eye to eye — in fact it is only through the expression of differences that effective problem-solving can take place. When aggression and conflict are totally suppressed they express themselves obliquely in all kinds of negative behaviour — withdrawal, cynicism, obstructiveness, and so on.

But too much conflict diverts or even disables the participants and so prevents problem-solving. Once I sat in on a meeting of senior company executives and taped the proceedings. The participants were all experienced committee men. Yet here are some of the violent remarks that were flying around the room:

'Don't take me for granted — I warn you, don't take me for granted.'
'You're always trying to attract attention to yourself. Why do you do that, David — trying for promotion?'
'You're deliberately twisting my words, as usual.'
'We won't explore your reasons for proposing that — they might prove embarrassing.'

And there was this tense little interchange:

A: We're forgetting item 8.
B: We dealt with that before you came.
A: I'm so sorry I was late.
B: We missed you terribly.
A: If you go on like this you'll finish up on the Board.

We've all been hit in meetings by this kind of verbal flak. It hurts, it damages relationships, and it disrupts the work of the group. No doubt some of the exploding passions are expressions of personality problems or stem from childhood difficulties. Sometimes one has the impression of early, hurtful relationships being re-enacted with people abusing the chairman and their parents in the same breath, so to speak. In therapeutic situations recovery often follows when the patient can be persuaded to adjust his attitudes towards his parents, siblings and others who ride around inside him like threatening spirits. *But in committee meetings the aim is not to cure the members but temporarily to counteract negative and disruptive behaviour so that the group can get on with the problem-solving.*

A properly trained chairman can play a major role in achieving this neutralising effect (see chapter 2). Senior managers and others responsible for supervising committees can also make a contribution by arranging for committee members to be trained in group dynamics, to attend sensitivity training courses, and so on. If a group can be stimulated to think about itself it can learn how to improve its performance. Thus some companies allow trained observers to sit in on committee meetings then discuss what happened with members afterwards. As in a guided missile system feedback helps to keep behaviour on target.

But what can you do, as an ordinary committee member, to counteract disruptive behaviour in meetings? Here are some suggestions:

1. *By recognising negative impulses in yourself AS negative impulses you can learn to control them* and not be drawn into damaging fights with others – except when there is genuine disagreement about a possible solution.

2. *Go into meetings with the attitude of being willing to learn. Be flexible. Look for areas of agreement.* Learn to bow to the general will. Because of the way that meetings work you will never have it all your own way.[1] Flat opposition and fighting talk merely trigger off angry reactions – the gentle approach is often more effective: 'I agree that a very strong case could be made out for that particular plan. I wonder if we could make it even stronger by a slight change of emphasis . . .'

[1] Engels pointed out that in history 'the final result always arises from conflict between many individual wills. . . . What each individual wills is obstructed by everyone else, and what emerges is something that no one willed.' This happens in meetings too. Hence the pained, consensus smile of the practised committee man.

According to Lewin groups change their minds by a three-stage process: (*a*) an 'unfreezing' of the previous attitude, (*b*) a change in attitude, and (*c*) the freezing of the new attitude. This means that if the committee is to accept your proposal it must first become convinced of the weaknesses in its present thinking. But this won't happen if you are too forceful and dogmatic because this will place you at a distance from the group and they won't 'hear' you correctly. They will reject your ideas if they are too alien to fit into the existing pattern of their thinking. To give your proposals a fair chance of being accepted start from where they already stand. Do this by gently encouraging them to make deductions about the gaps in their present thinking; and by inviting them to use *your* ideas to fill in the holes.

Effective participation in meetings doesn't mean getting your own way. Rather it means learning from others, accepting criticism and incorporating their ideas into your own proposals so that a superior decision is reached.

3. *By encouraging and conciliating when everyone else is growling and biting you can help to keep the group intact and moving towards a solution.* Here is how an ordinary member restored the peace at one meeting I attended:

A: I'm the chairman of that subcommittee and I should have been informed immediately of the authority's decision.

B: You're being completely unreasonable. I was informed myself only four days ago.

A: That doesn't matter. You've got my phone number. You've made me look a complete fool – and it's not the first time.

Peace-keeper: I can see that it must have been rather embarrassing for Mr A to find out about the decision through a third party. Though I think you'd agree, Mr A, that Mr B didn't have much time in which to act. I suppose the moral is to make it a ruling that in future the chairman of subcommittees should be informed as soon as possible of policy changes.

B: That's a fair point.

One member's positive remarks neutralised the negative feelings of the other two.

4. *Don't lecture, don't exhort, don't attack. People dig in their heels when they feel threatened and under attack.* To try to change a person's attitude by lecturing and direct instruction is to imply that he

is wrong: this is usually interpreted as attack and the usual defence is counter-attack.[1] Instead of threatening your committee colleagues by trying to prove how mistaken they are, try to show them in a pleasant and tactful way how they could strengthen their own proposals.

If you are convinced that a proposal is wrong and must be rejected at all costs, concentrate on exposing its defects. Discredit the idea by showing that it has been tried before unsuccessfully; that it's not a new idea; that it can't possibly work; or that it will be ruinously expensive to implement.

5. *Don't use or disagree with the Big Statement, the grand generalisation – of the 'employers are only interested in profits' type. Otherwise conflict will be generated out of mere words.* Wait for the specific instances, the concrete examples, because they contain the substance of what he is saying: 'Employers are only interested in profits . . .' (*Don't jump in: wait for the specific example*) '. . . you've only to look at the way management treated our last pay claim.' The argument turns out to be a very specific and factual one about a recent pay claim, not something wide and abstract. If specific examples are not forthcoming, ask for them.

Hesitate, in any case, before agreeing or disagreeing. Before you fire off a reply first restate his point in your own words to make sure you have understood his point. This reduces misunderstanding and sharpens your own contribution.

6. *Express your objections and disagreements tactfully. Make disagreement acceptable by complimenting the proposer on his objectives, or by first agreeing with some of the details of his proposal before disagreeing with the main theme.* This approach is necessary because even fair and impartial criticism can be interpreted as attack. The person concerned is likely to stop listening to the critic and instead work out an elaborate self-justification or a withering counterattack. If you don't mind risking a head-on clash try the full frontal assault: point out what the proposer is likely to gain if the proposal is accepted; hint at interest and partiality; stress the omissions and half-truths in his proposal. Your opponent will either fold his tenets and steal away into the night; or set about trying to destroy you.

---

[1] Verbal attack is resisted unless unleashed by a master of the art. When Wesley lashed his audience they wept and trembled and were converted.

Presenting a case

Expert presentation can sway even the toughest committee. In spite of the Roskill Commission's recommendation the British Cabinet — possibly the toughest-minded committee in the country? — decided to site London's new airport at Foulness, largely because of the brilliant presentation of its case by the anti-Cublington lobby. Excellent proposals die the death when presentation is weak; so if you wish your own proposals to be accepted in meetings the quality of presentation must match the quality of idea. Why should the nice guys always lose?

Imagine that you are a professional engineer working for a construction company and that you've worked out a scheme for reducing demolition costs by at least 5 per cent. You collect a lot of evidence to support your case: expert testimony, statistics, and so on. You bring your ideas into focus, set them down on paper. Only one obstacle remains: the company's Operations Committee, which must be convinced of the merits of your scheme before it can be placed before the board.

You go into the committee meeting and don't worry too much about presentation. In fact, you more or less throw your case at them, quite confident that the facts will speak for themselves. You're hurt and surprised when the committee reject your proposal. The company has lost an opportunity to reduce costs and your personal reputation has suffered.

A year later the committee accepts a very similar scheme presented (expertly) by another man.

It sounds an unlikely story but it really happened to a friend of mine. And I suspect that the experience is a fairly typical one. Often the facts refuse to speak for themselves. They tend to remain mute in committee meetings and only skilful communication can ram home their significance. *So when preparing a case for presentation to a committee plan it as you would plan a military campaign, with thoroughness, precision and careful timing. This will increase your chances of getting the proposal accepted. Study the chart on page 61 to get an idea of the logistics of the operation.*

Some reminders

1. Most managers need to work through committees to attain their goals. Attending meetings gives them the chance to make their

Preparing a case to present to a committee

PREPARATORY WORK

1 Thoroughly research your subject. Obtain all necessary information and supporting evidence. Remember that a single inaccuracy may destroy faith in your proposal.

2 Inform the Secretary of your intention to present an important proposal at the next meeting so that he can allow time for it and include it on the agenda.

4 Lobby your committee colleagues, explaining what you have in mind. This may enable you to capture the votes of the undecided centre block.

3 Prepare the opposition case so as to reduce your opponents' fire-power. You will be able to explain the disadvantages of your proposal yourself - and then explain how they can be overcome.

THE MEETING

6 During the meeting underline the main points and the main benefits of your proposal-remember that members have already read your memorandum which contained the details. Even at this late stage be willing to incorporate other people's ideas into the proposal -they may strengthen it or improve its chances of being accepted.

5 Circulate a memorandum to all members through the Secretary, stating your proposal in detail. Provide full supporting evidence.

Fig. 15:

talents available to the entire organisation and to influence the decision-makers.

2. When first joining a committee study the personal and group characteristics of your fellow-members. This will tell you which approaches will get the best results; which people and which topics need treating with special caution.

3. Make an impact in meetings by contributing early and frequently, and by thorough preparation which will compensate for your inexperience.

4. Prepare yourself for meetings by carefully reading all pre-circulated working documents and by thoroughly briefing yourself on important agenda items. Prepare brief notes for use as a speaking aid.

5. Help to reduce conflict in meetings by making encouraging and conciliatory remarks when people start snapping at each other.

6. Recognise negative impulses in yourself AS negative impulses and so learn to control them.

7. Be flexible in meetings, look for areas of agreement, be willing to incorporate other people's ideas into your own proposals.

8. Don't disagree with the Big Statement: wait for specific examples so that you don't start quarrelling over mere words.

9. Try to disagree with people tactfully if you wish to avoid aggressive counterattacks. For instance, first compliment the proposer on his objective then express doubt about the chances of his proposal's achieving it; or agree with details before rejecting the whole.

10. Expert presentation of a case greatly increases its chances of being accepted by a committee. Skilful advocacy and attractive packaging are needed to ram home the significance of the facts.

5 Power to Your Pen!

'Why not get to your employees through their noses?'

Written messages must be expressed, and understood, with clarity and precision, otherwise there can be a weakening of control within the organisation and a loss of goodwill outside. That is why writing managerial jargon is so dangerous: it may impress some readers but it mainly spreads uncertainty and confusion. Sometimes written communication is slow and costly and a message can be communicated more effectively by a telephone call or a short meeting or by visual methods.

Pompous expression is out of place in the modern world. Nobody who's tuned into a space conversation, for instance, can ever feel stuffy about language again: 'Razakeebazungadalasok, you bet. Oh boy! *Blip*.' It breaks all the rules of grammar but, oh boy, it communicates.

Today, overformal writing turns people off and causes communication breakdowns. Yet traces of commercialese or officialese cling like mildew to the communications sent by some managers. These are some of the forms it takes:

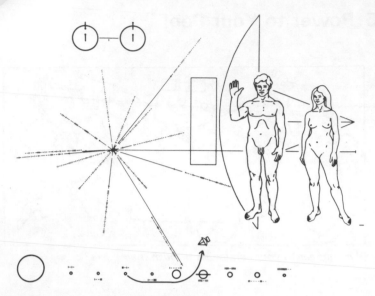

Fig. 16: *SPACE-AGE COMMUNICATION*
Pioneer 10 could be travelling through space 100 million years from now. On the off-chance that it might be intercepted by intelligent beings it is fitted with a plaque to tell where it came from. The pattern of lines represents the 14 pulsars of the Milky Way arranged to indicate the Sun as the home star of the launching civilisation. Binary numbers at the line-ends indicate present pulsar frequencies. These are running down at known rates so it might be possible to calculate when the space craft was launched. The bottom of the plaque shows the path of the space craft from Earth.

Assuring you of our best attention at all times (*omit*)
It would be greatly appreciated if (*omit*)
I have to inform you that (*omit*)
With reference to your communication of (*Thank you for your letter*)
At the present time (*Now*)
Under separate cover (*Later*)
Enclosed please find (*Here is*)

Musty relics like these have no place in business communications. Language is not working properly when it repels the reader and blurs the message.

Flights from plain language can prove expensive for a company. For instance, an important part of the manager's job is to remodel instructions and pass them down the line for action by operatives, technicians, salesmen and so on. And unless the message is expressed — and understood — with precision, jobs may be badly done, projects can be delayed, orders lost, and profits may go down.

Be simple

Stark simplicity is the best form of shock tactics in the war of words. Remember that out of the 1000 most used words only 36 have more than two syllables. Mark Twain was ahead of his time when he said, 'I never write "Metropolis" when I can get the same price for "City".' Beaverbrook advised his cub reporters to write for the *Daily Express* as if they were sending a cablegram at £1 a word. Being miserly with words forces you to pinpoint your meaning instead of circling round it. When the words are cut back the thoughts can be picked out with ease. This kind of writing demands much time and effort because, paradoxically, it's the simple style that takes most out of a writer. And there's no short cut. Either the writer sweats or the reader sweats. As Johnson said; 'What is written without effort is in general read without pleasure.'

Clipped, precise expression is a sure sign of clear thinking. After *The Times* reported that Rudyard Kipling was being paid £1 a word for an article he was writing some Oxford undergraduates sent him a £1 note with the request, 'Please send us one of your best words.' Kipling replied by postcard: 'Thanks.'

Simple statements jump off the page and into the mind. Using unnecessary words and phrases blunts your style and therefore your thinking and therefore your power to influence people in the way you intended.

This statement needs qualifying. As P. C. Wason and others have shown, in certain circumstances *too much* simplicity and verbal economy can have a boomerang effect and reduce understanding: recall from original manuscripts was superior to recall from precis versions. Padding can, in fact, boost understanding because, in effect, redundancies and repetition expose the reader to the same message several times over. The danger is, of course, that faced with this kind of style the reader will become bored and stop reading.

Short sentences with strong verbs keep the action going and solve most grammar and punctuation problems. Elaborate constructions make the prose plod. Complex sentence structure draws attention to itself — somehow interposes itself between the reader and the meaning. In the interests of good communication break the sentence you first thought of into its separate elements and make each of these into a short sentence. The result is that your message becomes clearer.

Laws of clear writing

1. *Simple declarative sentences are easier to understand than more complex forms.* Beginning a complex sentence with a dependent clause forces the reader to store the qualifying clause in his head until he comes to the information it is qualifying — i.e. the main clause.

Difficult: 'If the sentence has subordinate clauses — often introduced by "who", "which", "that" and "if", or lurking between dashes or parentheses — put them into separate sentences.'

Easier: 'Put any subordinate clauses into separate sentences. Such clauses are usually introduced by "who", "which", "that" or "if". Sometimes they lurk between dashes or parentheses.'

2. *Active constructions are easier to understand than passive*, as G. A. Miller and his associates at Harvard have shown. Passive constructions drain the life out of the page, although they are useful if you deliberately wish to create an impersonal style — for instance, so as to avoid any hint of personal criticism: 'This stage of the process was not properly completed . . .'

Difficult: 'It should be noted that forms are to be returned before the end of the period stated unless interest has been expressed in claiming special exemption.'

Easier: 'Kindly return forms before the end of the month OR request exemption.'

3. *Positive statements are easier to understand than negative statements*, which slow down understanding by turning the thought back-to-front ('The guarantee is invalid unless . . .'). Negatives are, by their nature, imprecise: 'We didn't go to London' — but where did they go? Experiments by Jones show that negative words in simple instructions can reduce the quality of the employee's performance; and Miller and McKean have shown that negative words (not, unless, except

etc.) delay understanding. But negatives do have their positive uses: some writers use them as buttresses against brashness and crudity. And they are useful when we wish to inhibit or prohibit the reader: 'NO OVERTAKING'.

Difficult: Do not disengage gears unless motor is OFF.
Easier: Keep gears engaged while motor is ON.

By keeping sentences ACTIVE, POSITIVE and SIMPLE in construction you help your reader to understand your communication with ease and precision.

Managerial jargon

Talking managerial jargon is less dangerous than *thinking* it.[1] Using jargon for thinking out a problem can surround it with a kind of insulating pad which rules out new approaches and imaginative solutions. Jargon blocks clear thinking. But by twisting out of the overused words and phrases you can often view a knotty problem from a new angle and see a way of solving it.

When a team of researchers tried to establish what three groups of people – industrial psychologists, personnel administrators and foremen – accepted as the meaning of several words commonly used by managers they found that none of the words produced a single agreed definition. Even within each group interpretations varied greatly. The words were:

attitude, communication, opinion, policy, personnel, practice, productivity, profit, quality, relations, research, scrap, security, standard, supervision, training, turnover.

Most managers use words like these all the time. They are a form of Byzantine expression, often admired yet often misinterpreted.

The trouble with managerial jargon is that it is imprecise, full of ambiguity. Phrases like 'market conurbations', 'appropriation variance' and 'maximum productivity' flow easily from the pen: but what exactly do they mean? Some words are accepted as having more than

---

[1] *Political* jargon has even more dangers: 'Defenceless villages are bombarded from the air, the inhabitants driven out into the countryside, the cattle machine-gunned, the huts set on fire ... this is called *pacification*.' See George Orwell's essay: 'Politics and the English Language'.

one meaning. For example, 'exposure' has a completely different meaning for the mountaineer, the photographer and the policeman, and usually the meaning is clear from the context. But the jargon words that managers use are ambiguous in any context. Such words are worse than useless: they can actually mean the wrong thing to other people.

Consider this simple example: 'It is now company policy to increase productivity.' To the manager this means: 'The board intends to produce more goods by means of improved technology'. But to the worker this means: 'A new company regulation requires all sections to produce as many goods in less time.' The moral, I suppose, is to assume nothing, choose your words with care and define every doubtful term and technical phrase. *If a great deal of technical terminology is used in written communications why not consider compiling and issuing a technological dictionary to every member of your staff?*

Here are the thirty words most frequently misunderstood by steelworkers, according to the Group Attitudes Corporation. Notice the number of abstract nouns (they have been described as the barbiturates of communication).

accrue embody inevitably
compute equitable injurious
concession excerpt jeopardy
contemplate facilitate magnitude
delete fortuitously modify
designate generate objectivity
deterioration impediment pursuant
detriment inadequate perpetuate
economic initiate subsequently
efficiency increment ultimate

In a study of 478 managers from various levels of Scottish industry fewer than 10 per cent of the specialist words and phrases commonly used in industry were satisfactorily understood.

Some managers seem to use jargon as a kind of verbal morning dress, worn with the idea of adding dignity and importance to one's communications. Is this why some managers talk about 'parameters' instead of 'limits'? Why ideas are 'meaningful' and people have 'charisma'? Why, 'hopefully', 'extrapolations' are made in attempts to 'maximise' 'cost-effectiveness'? It's easy writing nonsense like this because these in-words can be strung together in almost any combina-

tion you like and still form 'viable' sentences. What usually isn't so viable is the thought contained within the sentence: this is usually blurred.[1]

'Efficiency will inevitably be adversely affected unless there is a considerable modification of existing attitudes . . .' It is easy to write because the words have such wide and uncertain meanings. They are the sort of words that rise to the top of your brain when you're tired. Why do some managers use them all through the day?

Abstruse language masks fuzzy thinking. Reading managerial jargon in quantity is like being slowly knocked out with candyfloss. Some people enjoy juggling with words they don't really understand. But when they do this, they're involved in a word game, not communication.

Managers may be more successful than others in the organisation at understanding managerial jargon. People at the same level tend to use words in the same way and with the same meanings. But when a jargon-riddled message is expected to span levels the risk of a communication breakdown is severe. When an executive sends a jargon-filled memo to an operative the two men may seem to understand each other, they may even think they understand each other, yet confusion may well be the outcome.

Similarly, occupational jargon may actually speed up communication between people in the same department or within the same discipline. But the more narrowly specialised a man becomes the greater the danger that he will speak and think in an arcane language which nobody else understands. This is, admittedly, an advantage when the writer wishes to conceal his meaning from the receiver (company politics) or from himself (neurotic manager). And jargon can be extremely useful when there is a virtue in vagueness. An announcement of deadlock in wage negotiations can, if expressed in studiously ambiguous managerial jargon, allow everybody concerned in the dispute to interpret the statement as they please and so keep them patient while the talks drag on. A vaguely worded criticism of a section can spur it on to new efforts without damaging anybody's self-esteem.

[1] Some managers give the impression of being genuinely incapable of expressing themselves directly and simply. R. D. Laing refers to a type of psychiatric patient who deliberately uses 'obscurity and complexity as a smokescreen to hide behind' because 'any form of understanding threatens his whole defensive system' (*The Divided Self,* Tavistock Press, 1960, p. 175).

Annual reports should be readable

Here are extracts from two company annual reports. Which communicates its message the most clearly?

1. Price tendencies during the period under review continued the downward drift which had manifested itself at the commencement of the second quarter. Various financial measures have subsequently been taken by the different companies involved; it is hoped that these will allow capital expansion and so succeed in effecting an improvement in the group's trading position during the current financial year. As the tables below will indicate . . .

Prose like this lives in an elephantine world of its own. It's as if the writer has been locked in a board room all his life, in telephone contact with an investment analyst but with no knowledge whatsoever of the preferences of the people he should be writing his report for — the public. The basic message is there but it is castrated by the dead abstractions — 'tendencies', 'manifested itself', 'various financial measures'. Why couldn't the writer simply say: 'Prices began falling in July and they have continued to fall. But we have raised a new loan which will allow us to expand.' Contrast the second passage:

2. Highlight of the year has been the introduction of the Morris Marina range of cars. They were well received and sold steadily from the start. Car sales have increased during the year, likewise the number of used vehicles sold. Light vans have been in steady supply throughout. The Parts and Service division had a good year. . . . But the current year will be difficult and profits will be hard to find.

The writer has broken right away from board room doubletalk. Using simple unpretentious language he's made sure that his message will get through to the reader. Why shouldn't *your* company's annual report be plainer in language, sprightlier in presentation and aimed at turning the turned-off public on?

Hemingway once said: 'People think I'm an ignorant bastard who doesn't know the ten-dollar words. There are older and better words. . . . Remember, anybody who pulls his erudition and education on you hasn't any.' Before a man can abandon the managerial prose perhaps he first needs to abandon the managerial pose.

How readable are your communications?

R. Gunning's Fox Index is one of the best-known schemes for assessing readability. All you have to do is calculate the average sentence length, assess the number of words in your sample which have three or more syllables, then add these figures together and multiply the result by 0.4. The answer, for some reason, indicates the number of years' education needed to read the passage with ease.

Here is a quicker, easier way of checking on the readability of your own written communication. Take a 200-word sample from one of your letters or reports then

1. For each sentence over 20 words long give yourself 5 points.
2. For each passive verb give yourself 5 points.
3. For each word over two syllables long give yourself 2 points.

Then check your total score against this rating scale:

Below 60: very easy to read.
60–100: fairly readable but presenting some difficulties to less educated readers.
100–140: quite difficult to read.
Over 140: difficult and obscure.

Find out where most of your points are coming from: those are the aspects of your style which are reducing readability. As a final check on readability ask yourself these questions:

1. Am I clear about my *objective* whenever I put pen to paper? What is it? Is a written communication the best way of achieving it?
2. Is the communication *reader oriented* in both content and form?
3. Does the *headline* explain the relevance of the message to the reader? And does the first paragraph explain this relevance in greater detail?
4. Is the communication as simple and clear as *constant rewriting* can make it?
5. Have I used *graphics* to maximum advantage?
6. Have I used *signposting devices* to make the message easy to follow, e.g. listing the items to be covered and frequent headings and subheadings?
7. Have I *repeated the main points* to ensure clear understanding and have I stated exactly what action I want the reader to take or conclusions that I want him to reach?

Limitations of written communication

The limitations of written communication are revealed by what happened in one northern wool mill. Sales had been low for several years. Low morale was reflected in high absenteeism and high labour turnover. Then a rumour began to spread to the effect that redundancy plans were being drawn up and that half the employees would lose their jobs. The board decided to scotch the rumour. It drew up a statement which emphasised that all jobs were secure and that trading prospects were good. Copies of the statement were posted on all notice boards. But the rumours persisted. A week later the chief shop steward asked the Personnel Manager for full details of the redundancy scheme!

Written communication had failed. Eventually the board hit on a more effective way of convincing the employees. A series of depart-

Export of Television Receivers

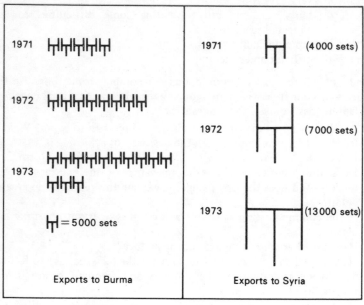

Fig. 17: *By using symbols appropriate to the fact being represented pictograms communicate statistical information quickly and simply. Quantity is usually shown by repeating the symbol but it can also be shown by increasing the size of the symbol.*

mental meetings was held with at least one director attending each meeting. Everybody attending was handed a copy of the board's previous statement, and the director explained just what was meant by *this* point, what the facts were behind *that* statement. Then the employees asked questions and the director tried to answer them. 'As a result of this face-to-face communication', one manager claimed, 'confidence in management seemed to increase.' Certainly the rumours disappeared and productivity picked up.

When the two sides of industry are far apart written communication is a poor bridge-builder: the men who read the communications lack trust and confidence in the men who write them. When Revans studied communication in the coal industry he noted that many types of written communication had been used by management — memos, leaflets, even a personal letter from the Prime Minister — in trying to persuade miners to raise their output. But output stayed low: written communication proved to be a blunt instrument. Revans concluded that the mere provision of information did not succeed in modifying

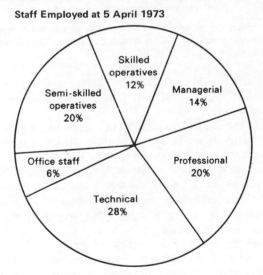

Staff Employed at 5 April 1973

Fig. 18: *Pie-charts are concise and dramatic. They look simple and non-technical and so are useful for communicating technical and financial information to laymen. They show how component parts add up to make a total.*

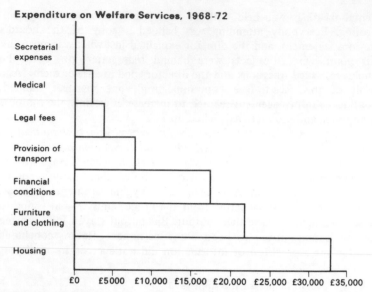

Fig. 19: *Bar charts are an effective way of driving home a comparison or contrast between items: the visual effect points up the differences or similarities.*

the underlying attitude of mistrust upon which credibility seems to be based. And credibility and trust spring not from written messages but from friendly face-to-face contact.

So remember the limitations of written communication and experiment with alternative methods. Experiments at the Canadian Broadcasting Corporation's studio's in Montreal showed that print ranked fifth in order of impact on an average audience, behind television, film, radio and oral communication. *A written message is easy to ignore and easy to misunderstand. Its effectiveness depends on the writer's skill and the reader's motivation and education – and often, in industrial settings, at least one of these factors is missing.*

A way of avoiding some of the pitfalls of written communication is to make more use of visual methods. Charts, graphs and diagrams offer less scope for misinterpretation than words. Moreover, much more information is conveyed per square inch of paper than by words. Yet in spite of this concentration, it is easy for the reader to visualise information presented graphically and this is a useful method for

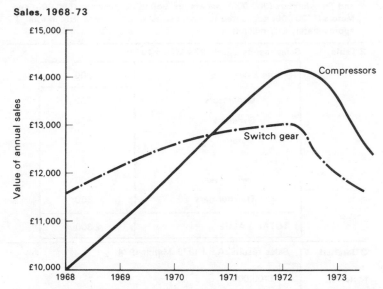

Sales, 1968-73

Fig. 20: *Graphs give a quick impression of a general trend or the major features. For instance, in this graph the sudden decline in sales over the past year immediately commands attention.*

getting complicated technical information across to non-technical people, as the pictogram, Fig. 17, shows. Each type of chart or graph performs one particular function best – e.g. statistical tables are best for the precise and full reporting of data, graphs are very effective for showing trends, column charts are best for comparing performance, sales or production at different periods, and so on. The art of graphical communication consists of using each form of presentation for doing the job it does best.

Even colours can be used to bypass words. For instance, oranges and reds suggest warmth; reds suggest energy or violence; blues and greens are cool, restful colours. A well-chosen colour scheme in a workshop or office can do more to improve the emotional climate than any number of memos or meetings.

Or why not get to your employees through their noses? Today you can buy twenty or thirty instant print-on smells. Why shouldn't your early-morning memos release the aroma of fresh-roast coffee as they land on the desk?

1 Written communication

During the period April 1973 to March 1974 sales totalled £2.8 millions, compared with £2.2 millions for the previous year. Export sales were valued at approximately £1.1 millions and consisted of sales of Switchgear (800,000) and Transformers (300,000). Generators (950,000), Dynamos (650,000) and Motors (£100,000) accounted for home sales which were worth, in total, approximately £1.7 millions

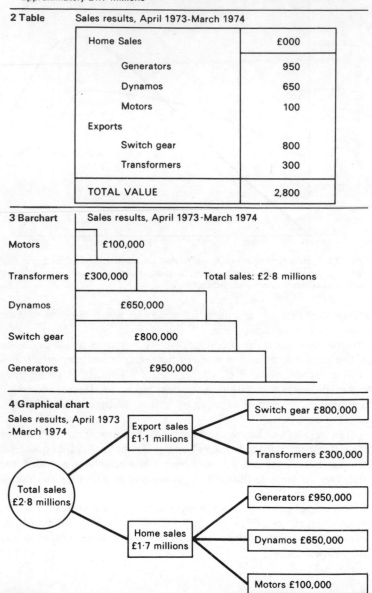

2 Table   Sales results, April 1973-March 1974

Home Sales	£000
Generators	950
Dynamos	650
Motors	100
Exports	
Switch gear	800
Transformers	300
TOTAL VALUE	2,800

3 Barchart   Sales results, April 1973-March 1974

Motors £100,000

Transformers £300,000   Total sales: £2·8 millions

Dynamos £650,000

Switch gear £800,000

Generators £950,000

4 Graphical chart

Sales results, April 1973-March 1974

Total sales £2·8 millions

Export sales £1·1 millions — Switch gear £800,000; Transformers £300,000

Home sales £1·7 millions — Generators £950,000; Dynamos £650,000; Motors £100,000

Fig. 21: *Four ways of communicating the same information. Which is the most effective?*

Fig. 22: *Signs and symbols can communicate better than words in a busy street — and also in the fast world of business where people often have to go through the right door or push the right button without stopping to read. When making signs and posters you need to think in a new way about clearness and visibility. For optimum visibility use the following colour combinations: black on white, black on yellow, dark blue on white, grass green on white.*

Key points

1. Simple declarative sentences are easier to understand than more complex forms; active constructions are easier to understand than passive; positive constructions are easier to understand than negative.
2. Many words widely used in industry — policy, productivity, security, turnover etc. — have different meanings for different groups of people. So choose your words with care and define every doubtful term.

77

3. Abstruse language often masks fuzzy thinking. When the language is starkly simple the thought stands out more sharply.
4. Paradoxically, a simple style demands more time and effort than a long-winded style.
5. *Thinking* managerial jargon inhibits new approaches and imaginative solutions to problems. *Writing* it produces confusion in both the writer's and the reader's mind.
6. Jargon can speed up communication between people within the same discipline or at the same level. But it causes communication breakdowns between people of different levels and disciplines.
7. Companies' annual reports are too often written for the investment analyst. To reach a wider public you may need to make your annual report simpler in language, sprightlier in presentation.
8. When the two sides of industry are far apart written communication is a poor bridge-builder. Credibility and trust spring not from written messages but from frequent face-to-face communication.
9. Charts, graphs, diagrams, posters etc. offer less scope for misinterpretation than words. And it is easy for the reader to visualise information presented graphically so this is a useful method for getting complicated technical information across to non-technical people.
10. What kinds of charts would be used to show the following: (*a*) rising production, (*b*) one year's export figures for *six* different commodities, (*c*) proportions of a domestic budget?

6 The Writing Chores
Memos, Short Reports, Letters

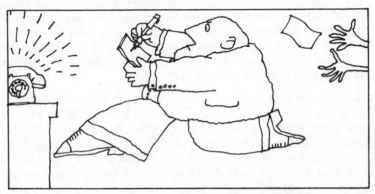

'Memos tend to be written in a rush between phone calls or meetings.'

Every time a manager writes a memo or a short report or a letter there is an underlying objective — some action or response that he is trying to trigger off, some order or invitation or decision that he is trying to engineer. A man with the ability to win such responses through his written communications is a valuable capital asset to a company. Outlined here are some ways in which this ability can be developed. Aspects covered include the importance of finding the right tone, the careful selection of material, and devices for arranging the material so that the thought stands out in sharp focus.

A quick way with memos

Imagine you are in charge of a department where, several times in recent weeks, an expensive new duplicator has been carelessly used and damaged. You decide to take action and dictate a memo for circulation to all your staff. You do this and the memo is typed out and placed on your desk. You read it through:

> Every member of this department has already received a memorandum which explains the precise procedures for operating the new dry copier. It is therefore with considerable surprise that I have noted that these procedures have been ignored on several occasions in the last few weeks, the machine having been used for excessive periods without being allowed to cool, and without being switched off after use. I should be obliged if you would ensure that the correct procedures are observed henceforth.

As soon as you have read this through you begin to have doubts. The style is long-winded and pompous. The reader is not reminded what the 'correct procedures' are. And the tone is wrong because you sound as if you are talking to stupid and irresponsible children. You realise that if this memo is sent out relations with your employees will suffer. So you try another approach and, at the second attempt, this is what you produce:

From: Manager, Despatch Dept
To: All staff   *Date:* 2 October

NEW COPYING MACHINE: OPERATING INSTRUCTIONS

1. All staff are welcome to use the new dry copier which was recently installed in the General Office.
2. The machine can be rather temperamental so it is important to keep to the following procedure when using it:

   A. Do not use the machine for longer than 30 minutes at a time.
   B. After use, allow the machine to cool for *at least five minutes* before using again.
   C. Make sure the switch is turned to OFF after use.

Please speak to me if you have any queries about the machine.

The second version is better than the first in every way. The style is simpler and more direct. The material is arranged efficiently so that the thought stands out more sharply. The tone is far more pleasant. This memo will probably win your staff's full cooperation: the first version would only have produced resentment and hostility.

The second version is clearly superior yet in many companies it's the first that gets written and sent. One reason is that memos tend to be written in a rush, between phone calls or meetings. If only there were a way of writing memos quickly yet clearly and precisely. Well, fortunately there is. No doubt there are several. But the following method should enable you to produce crisp, clear memos with no time wasted.

1. *Be selective.* Make the memo short and direct, while maintaining a pleasant tone. Include only information that the reader needs to know. Get straight into the message with no introductory or closing flourishes. Clip and compress your message by leaving out all unnecessary details. Use graphs, drawings, diagrams if these help you to tell your story quickly and clearly.

2. *Use short numbered paragraphs.* This device forces you to unravel thoughts before you put pen to paper, compels you to break down a complicated idea into its component parts which can then be arranged in order of importance.

Numbering paragraphs makes the memo easier to write and easier to read. The reader can follow your message step by step in a logical sequence. This makes it easy to understand, easy to remember, easy to act on.

If the memo is a fairly long and complicated one it is easier to follow if broken into sections. Give each section a heading, with numbered paragraphs below.

3. *Add a heading.* The reader can then tell, by glancing at the heading, what you are writing about. The heading also helps the filing clerk to find the right file for it.

4. *Quickly revise.* If time allows, quickly rewrite the memo to make sure that the final effect is one of crispness and clarity, and that you've not been too abrupt, too supercilious etc. Cut out unnecessary words and phrases. Simplify sentences. Polish the phrasing.

A word of caution. Don't send memos to people who don't really need them. The 'copy to everybody' approach wastes a lot of people's time and is extremely expensive. If you don't require a reply to your memo show this by adding 'For Information Only' at the top.

In most companies memos are the most widely used, and at the same time most widely misused, method of communication. They form part of the general impression that a manager makes on his subordinates and his colleagues. They also provide a permanent record of important instructions and policies. (Memos stating policies need to be written with great care and precision: for months or years ahead they will be relied on to settle disputes about what was said and decided, and to help with the decision-making.)

Well-written memos add to the climate of professionalism in the department. That is why it is worth training your subordinates – and yourself – to write them with clarity, courtesy and precision.

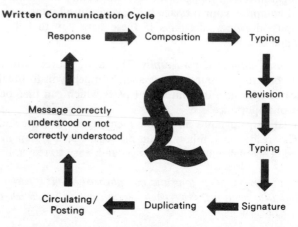

Fig. 23: *Communicating by letter or memo can be a slow and costly process, as this chart shows. Mistakes and delays can occur at any stage in the cycle. Often a telephone call or a short meeting enables you to get across more information and to answer more questions than an entire series of written messages.*

Short reports get quick attention

President Eisenhower had a rule that reports should not exceed one sheet of foolscap. And Churchill sent a memo to all government departments in 1940 which said:

I ask my colleagues to see to it that their reports are shorter.
1. The aim should be reports which set out the main points in a series of short, crisp paragraphs.
2. If the report relies on a detailed analysis of some complicated factors, or on statistics, these should be set out in the appendix.

Most senior managers are just as allergic to paper as Eisenhower or Churchill were. Probably *you* prefer to receive short, easy-to-read reports from your staff. And your boss, in turn, is certain to prefer short, simple reports from you. Something he can deal with on the spot, before the telephone rings or an important visitor arrives.

Short reports usually get quick attention while longer screeds lie on the desk unread. Short reports give senior managers the information they want in a nutshell and save dozens of telephone calls, memos, meetings. Sometimes longer, more formal reports are unavoidable. But a short informal report might be more effective in the following instances:

· The General Manager asks you to jot down your impressions of how efficiently a new section is operating.

· The Personnel Director asks for your comments on present recruitment methods.

· You don't like a new despatch procedure and wish to explain your views to the board.

In each case you might decide that a short informal report is the best tool for the job because you want your ideas to be considered *now*, while they are still fresh. You hope for quick results.

If the subject really does require more than one or two pages, why not split the subject into two parts and write a crisp, short report on each? Hand in the second a week after entering the first. Two short documents will probably get quick attention whereas a longer report might be tossed to one side, to be dealt with when time permits.

Lead with your ace

When writing a short report place your strongest points at the beginning because that's where they will make the most impact. Back up each one with three or four well-chosen supporting points: these will have more effect than a whole posse of weak riders.

Arrange your material under three of four subheadings, with numbered paragraphs below each one. Numbering the paragraphs makes it easier to discuss the report in a meeting or over the phone. Tell your story with the help of drawings, graphs, photographs — any graphical method which saves words and makes your meaning clearer.

Above all, angle the report to the reader's point of view. Show how your findings or recommendations will help him improve his depart-ment's work methods or enable him to cut overheads or to save on raw materials. Give him the information HE wants, not the information that interests YOU.

Final check

Check through the report and

- Cut out all unnecessary phrases and words;
- Cut down sentence length and paragraph length;
- Remove any information that your reader will not find useful;
- Cut the clichés. Don't raise your sights. Let's not face it. You haven't checked and double-checked any calculations, have you?

A short report doesn't need an elaborate structure. If it's less than, say, 500 words long why not simply write it out in memo form? If it's longer than about 2,000 words perhaps a formal report would be more appropriate.

But a short report of between 500 and 2,000 words should need no more than three or four sections, each with its own subheading. Check that these three or four sections are arranged in the most logical order, with any conclusions or recommendations coming in the last section. Once you've done this, hand it in and expect a speedy reaction.

The finished, hand-in version should look something like this:

From: A. Rogers
To: General Manager
Copies to: All supervisory staff   *Date:* 1 October 1973

ASSESSMENT OF PRESENT RECRUITMENT METHODS

1. *First paragraph* stating your terms of reference, i.e. the instructions given by the General Manager, or your purpose in submitting the report.

2. *Second paragraph:* succinct outline of present methods of recruit-ment, presented factually and with supporting evidence.

3. *Third paragraph:* possible changes, with a brief explanation of the advantages of each suggested change, together with supporting evidence.

4. *A final, clinching paragraph* showing how the company would benefit overall by accepting your entire package and with any financial benefits highlighted.

Writing effective letters

Every business communication is purposive. There is always some underlying objective in communicating, some action or response that the communicator is trying to trigger off. An ineffective communication, by definition, fails to evoke a response; or it causes a response that the sender didn't intend – an angry outburst, a cancelled order, a 'No' instead of a 'Yes'. That is why a good letter writer is a valuable asset to a company. A manager who can write effective letters wins the right responses. Therefore he is a goodwill-builder and, indirectly, a profit-builder. Every day he 'sells' the company and its products. Every letter he writes represents an opportunity to influence people favourably: every letter carelessly written represents an opportunity lost. Putting words on paper is hard enough: the ability to do it so that people are persuaded or motivated in the way you intend is a rare skill.

The surest way of avoiding the wrong response is to plan every letter carefully. Routine letters – acknowledgements and covering letters, say – may require only a few seconds' thought about arrangement and phrasing. But more important letters may require hours of careful planning and drafting. Most of us have to slave to get an important letter exactly right. My own letters become focused and clear only after several successive drafts. A quick and reliable way of replying to somebody else's letter is to underline the points to be answered then make brief marginal notes against the underlined items. Finally, write or dictate the reply direct from the notes.

A company is judged by the letters it sends. Correspondence is the only direct link that hundreds or thousands of people have with the company. According to what the letters they receive say and how they say it, so the company and its products and its policies are praised or condemned.

One company was shocked when it discovered that every letter it sent was costing £1 to produce. But the cost of producing a letter is nothing compared with the cost of the goodwill that can be lost when letters are written hastily and carelessly.

An approach to letter-writing

People become expert letter writers as a result of wide experience of business and people and after years of trial and error. But you may be able to improve on your present performance by using the following method. When writing a letter:

1. First assemble all the material you need — company policies, files, previous correspondence etc. Extract any details or references you require.

2. Add to this information any ideas on the subject that come to mind.

3. Group all these items of information under headings. Arrange the groups in a logical sequence.

4. Write a draft letter from these notes — change them into continuous prose. Don't worry about polish and precise expression at this stage — these qualities can be added later. *Aim to give your correspondent the information he most wants in the opening paragraph: the proposition, the result of the application, the state of the negotiations, and so on. Close the letter by stating what action you want him to take and explain how he'll benefit by taking this action.*

5. Quickly revise. Remove parasite words and phrases, and strike out any information that the reader doesn't really require. Rephrase sentences that sound wrong or that are ambiguous or unclear. Simplify and sharpen the argument. Remove any trite opening or closing comment of the 'Assuring you of our best attention' kind.

6. Finally, write or dictate the letter, making any simplifications or improvements as you go along. Aim at a final version which is crisp, clear and courteous: the sort of letter you like to receive yourself. The letter below has all these qualities:

6th May 1973

Dear Tom,

Thank you for your letter of May 1st and for the samples of the special 'Anniversary' ware. These look good, and as I am now on speaking terms with my General Manager I have passed them on to him for his comments.

The position now is that as soon as I receive his approval I shall need a precise estimate from **you of the cost of** *two thousand complete sets*, together with discount terms and a firm delivery date.

With luck, we should be able to sign the contract before the end of next week. If so, we should like to include a clause giving us an option on a further five thousand sets for delivery before the end of the year.

Please let me have your reactions.

Yours,
Nigel

Replying to complaints

Replying by letter to complaints needs special care. A tactless or aggressive reply can create an enemy or make the complainant go elsewhere with his grievance: if this is outside the company real damage may be done. So use the letter as an opportunity to promote goodwill and correct a misunderstanding. Thank your correspondent for drawing your attention to the error. Explain why it happened and what you intend to do about it. Be sympathetic. Try to solve his problem. Don't try to finesse him.

Letters of refusal

It is difficult to write letters of refusal without causing offence. Norman Shidle's 'Kiss 'em, Kick 'em, Kiss 'em' method sidesteps this danger:

1. Find a way of complimenting your correspondent. Tell him what an interesting idea it is, or how interested you'd been to meet him, or how pleased you were that he'd asked you.
2. Say no plainly, with reasons.
3. Offer a solution or partial solution to his problem: another way in which he could tackle his problem, a more suitable time, someone else he might contact. Make him feel that his efforts haven't been wasted and that he has something to thank you for even if it isn't what he had hoped for in the first place.

Dear Mr Sturdy,

I'm sure that the expedition to the Sahara that you are planning will be a great success and that you will have no difficulty in finding several firms wishing to sponsor it.

Unfortunately, this company has already sponsored two expeditions this year and I'm sure the board would not consider supporting a third.

If you decide to organise another expedition next year I hope that you will get in touch with us again because we might be able to give a different answer.

Yours sincerely,
N. George
Personnel Director

The importance of good presentation

Indifferent layout and presentation can ruin the effect of a competently written letter. Wide margins, balanced blocks of type, good quality paper and envelope — all contribute to a favourable impression. There is no one correct method of layout. Fashions change constantly. For instance, 'block form' was fashionable a few years ago, with every line beginning at the lefthand margin. At the moment, 'Dear Mr Smith/ Yours sincerely' (in the US, 'Dear Tom/Very truly yours') seems to have edged out the more formal 'Dear Sir/Yours faithfully'. But for how long?

Some firms sidestep many problems of arrangement and expression, and at the same time speed up the letter-writing process, by issuing form-letter manuals to their executives. These contain model letters and paragraphs: the writer simply lists the code numbers of the letters or paragraphs he wishes to use and hands these to the typist.

An effective way of identifying weak aspects of company or departmental correspondence is to see copies of all letters sent out over a two-week period. Characteristic shortcomings such as poor layout and design, careless typing and so on, are quickly identified, and eradicated by appropriate training.

Dictating letters

Efficient dictation requires both careful preparation and good delivery. Lack of preparation means false starts, long pauses and rambling sentences: on paper the result is long, loose letters which waste the reader's time and pile up the transcription bills.

Prepare for dictation. First gather together all relevant files and extract the information you need. Jot down key words and phrases on a sheet of paper then shuffle these into the most logical order. Use these notes to dictate from. The natural thing to do when dictating is to speak by the thought rather than by the sentence but this is a habit you have to discipline yourself out of because it results in very long and clumsy sentences. So develop the habit of consciously using short sentences and saying 'full stop' after each one. As you listen to yourself dictating, these sentences may sound truncated and abrupt, but on paper they will look crisp and clear.

Say 'paragraph' and 'quote/unquote' as often as these are required, and spell out all awkward words so that you don't have to send the letter back for retyping. To capture the right tone, visualise the reader of your letter. Imagine that he is sitting opposite you and that it is to him rather than to the typist that you are speaking.

Letters by remote control
Centralised dictating is one of the quickest and easiest ways of cutting office costs, because a number of shorthand typists can be replaced by a smaller number of audio-typists. The Nabisco Foods factory in Welwyn Garden City used to employ about thirty secretaries, shorthand typists and copy typists. Since installing centralised dictation facilities there is a total of eight audio-typists and one supervisor handling the typing for about a hundred executives. The British Rail offices at Derby have recorded output figures of 800 lines of typing a day compared with an average 350 lines previously. At National Carriers' London offices six audio-typists transcribe the dictation of any of the 350 staff.

There are two forms of centralised dictation, tandem and bank. The tandem system gives each typist a two-machine unit: one accepts dictation while the other is used for transcribing. The bank system incorporates a number of machines into which all dictation is fed. A supervisor removes recorded material and gives it to any typist in the centre to transcribe. Some systems, such as IBM's, provide microphones for dictators, but most use the internal telephone service. Control is through push-button, dialling or a combination of both. There is usually also a hunting device so that the dictator can find out which recorder in the bank is free.

Apart from astonishing improvements in productivity which quickly recoup the initial outlay there are many other benefits:

· Executives can deal with letters and memos as soon as they are at hand. There is no need to carry an argument or information in your head until the shorthand typist arrives.
· Everybody has dictation facilities on his desk. The service is prompt and efficient and the cost is low.

- There are fewer problems because of absence of peak periods.
- Typists have a steady flow of work channelled onto their desks.
- Most systems allow dictation facilities outside of office hours.

Getting dictators to use the facility efficiently can be a major problem. But most of the well-known manufacturers have a good record of consultancy and follow-up services and most are prepared to train not only dictators but also typists and supervisors to use the system effectively. Another snag is that audio-typing pools are not popular and many girls would rather leave their jobs than be moved into one. According to the National Institute of Industrial Psychology the following approaches reduce the dissatisfaction:

- Keep the typing pool as small as possible. Two small pools are better than one large one.
- Give regular planned breaks from work.
- Make sure that supervision is effective.
- Give as much variety to the girls as possible, including clerical jobs.
- Adequate training is very important.
- Explore the possibility of employing part-timers in the pool.

Key points

Memos
1. Compress the message by leaving out inessential details; by leaving out introductory and closing flourishes; and by using graphical devices to tell your story quickly and simply.
2. Use short numbered paragraphs. This device forces the *writer* to break down his idea into its component parts and makes it easier for the *reader* to understand, remember and act on the memo.
3. When time allows, revise the memo: simplify sentences, cut out unnecessary words and phrases, aim at a final effect of crispness and clarity.

Short reports
4. A short report gives the reader the information he wants in a nutshell; yet it may save dozens of memos, telephone calls and meetings. Moreover, short reports usually get quick attention while longer, formal reports lie on the desk, unread.

5. Arrange the material for your report in three or four sections, each with its subheading. State any conclusions or recommendations you wish to make in the final section.
6. Use any graphical devices which would make your meaning clearer or help to explain complicated points.
7. Angle the report to the reader's point of view. Show how your findings or recommendations will help him to cut overheads, find extra profits etc. Give him the information *he* wants rather than the information that interests *you.*

Letters
8. A letter may have to be redrafted several times before it is clear and focused.
9. Give your correspondent the information he most wants in the opening paragraph — the proposition, the result of the application, the offer.
10. Close the letter by stating the action you want him to take and explain how he will benefit by taking this action.
11. Could you speed up the letter-writing process in your department without any loss of quality by introducing a form-letter manual containing model letters and paragraphs?
12. Could you improve the quality of departmental correspondence by seeing copies of letters sent out over a two-week period so that you can identify shortcomings and arrange appropriate training?

7 Communicating with Non-Specialists Writing Formal Reports

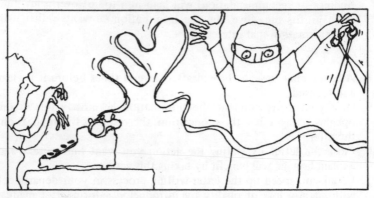

'You'll see malignant constructions which require immediate surgery.'

Any fool can make a complicated subject *sound* complicated but it takes skill and judgment to express it simply. The ability to do this is invaluable in report writers, for although formal reports usually deal with highly complex material they are first and foremost communication exercises, written to convince or persuade people. When writing a report, how should you arrange the material for maximum impact? How can you make sure that the non-specialist or the specialist from another discipline will grasp your argument? These are some of the questions which this chapter tries to answer.

Hundreds of reports are written every year in most big firms. There are routine reports giving production and stock figures, or the latest sales results. There are annual reports, progress reports, reports about research or labour turnover or new processes. Some reports are written by specialists wishing to explain the work they are doing to their own kind and to others. This variety explains why, in spite of hundreds of books and articles on the subject, there is no one sure way of learning how to write a report. The right way depends on who the report is for and what it is about.

For instance, the company may have a preferred format: many companies provide printed report forms to ensure uniform presentation. Again, the manager who calls for the report may have his own whims about style and presentation which you will need to take into account. If you write the report on your own initiative you may decide to submit it in memo form with very little structure at all. Or you may find that style and presentation are largely irrelevant, as when you contribute to the company's annual report: sections or departments often submit their own reports which are then compressed and collated, a final version being written up by an advertising agency.

The effects of a clumsily written report can range from exasperation to downright misinformation. To avoid these effects you need to know exactly who will be reading it and the use they plan to make of it. Suppose your boss calls for a report on how well a new despatch procedure is working. From your knowledge of the man you realise that he will be less interested in what staff feel than in what customers feel. You also know about his fad for treble-spacing and his hatred of statistics. You do a little probing and discover that he'll be discussing your report with *his* boss who is famous for favouring the middle way, the compromise solution. Armed with this kind of knowledge about the readers you can almost leave your report to write itself.

If you know that the reader is interested only in the practical consequences for his department of your investigation, these will be the aspects you emphasise at the beginning and again at the end of the report. If the report describes a series of laboratory experiments and is meant for the Research Director, you will make sure it contains a very detailed, stage-by-stage account of the research and gives full details of the findings presented in the form of a formal research document.

Be reader-oriented. Don't include any information which is surplus to the reader's requirements. If all he wants is a guideline to help him reach a particular decision, don't offer him a mass of test results and pages of statistics. If the report is to be considered by a committee of laymen, include adequate background information, avoid jargon, and stress your conclusions and recommendations.

Generally speaking, senior managers want a general not a detailed picture and also a full analysis of the financial implications. Middle managers are more likely to be interested in the mechanics of your investigation, the details, the technical feasibility.

Write your report with the needs of the reader clearly in mind. Decision-makers have to be sold not told. This means anticipating their doubts and objections and answering them. So begin by getting your terms of reference completely clear:

- Exactly who is to read it?
- What is the precise purpose; what will it be used for?
- Exactly what information is required?
- Is a detailed stage-by-stage account of your investigation appropriate, or an outline account together with recommendations and conclusions?

Investigate!

Once you know the answers to these questions give yourself a time limit in which to write the report. This might vary from half an hour for a routine report containing production figures, to many months of systematic investigation for a report which could lead to a major change of process or policy. *But having set yourself a time limit in relation to the importance of the report, be sure to keep to it.*

I strongly recommend a preliminary literature search at this stage to ensure that the work has not already been done and written up. A friend of mine who works on a copper mine spent several months investigating the growth of 'nodules' in pipes carrying fluids which contained copper. He completed his investigation, wrote his report and handed it to the Plant Superintendent. A few days later he was shown a report which had been forwarded from another mine in the group. This document, which covered the same ground and reached precisely the same conclusions, had been written a year earlier. Presumably it would have come to light if only my friend had taken the precaution of doing a literature search before getting down to work.

Probe into the files of your own company. Approach other companies for advice. Technical information is being produced at such a rate that keeping up to date can be extremely difficult, but there are Abstracts of new ideas and publications – e.g. *Science Abstracts* issued monthly by the Institution of Electrical Engineers and dealing with publications in many branches of science. The *World List of Scientific*

Publications (Butterworth) lists 5000 scientific and technical periodicals and shows which libraries keep them. The *Technical Book Review* lists the most important new books. Glancing at the book reviews in the technical Press is a good way of keeping in touch with the latest ideas. Trade catalogues, issued by many companies, often contain very useful information such as weights, dimensions of products etc.

Of course, firsthand information has more impact and validity than facts collected from books and magazines. The usual ways in which firsthand information is collected are by direct observation and experiments, interviews, questionnaires, telephone conversations, letters of enquiry. Questionnaires are the cheapest way of collecting information from a lot of people; interviewing is more suitable for 'in-depth' probing. Keep notes of how each item of information was obtained so that you can quote your sources in the report.

Finally, don't rely too much on any one source. The wider you spread your net the more polished and balanced the final result. (Taking material from one writer is plagiarism: taking it from many is research.)

As your material swells you'll need to start arranging it in separate folders and under separate headings. Once you have more than enough material, get rid of the surplus fat. Go systematically through each folder and get rid of irrelevant, repetitious and uninteresting material. The information that is left is the raw material from which you will write up your report. REMEMBER: *Don't write out the report until the subject has been as thoroughly investigated as your time-allowance will permit, and only after all irrelevant and uninteresting information has been weeded out.*

The first draft

If your report is hastily written and carelessly presented it may be ignored by the people who should read it. Don't write it in a rush. Now that you've assembled all the parts of the puzzle allow yourself enough time to put them together properly. 'A piece of writing meditated apparently without progress for months or years may suddenly take shape and words; and in this state long passages may be produced which require little or no retouch.' The words are T. S. Eliot's. He was talking about poetry, but they apply just as strongly to report writing. Provided you give yourself ample time the actual writing out will come easily in the end. Work on your report daily over as long a period as

it allows: every day the overall argument and conclusions
clearer shape in your mind.

p in the writing-out process is to draft a contents list using
ings on the folders, perhaps, as a starting point. Doing this
forces you to unscramble your thoughts and to start looking for an
overall pattern and progression.

After writing the contents list, collect all the material you intend to
use in the first section. Begin to work on this material: group similar
bits of information together, then combine these small collections into
larger groups. Arrange these large groups into the most logical order so
that, following one on the other, they tell a continuous and coherent
story. Relegate to appendixes all statistics and technical data which
would slow down the action and spoil the clarity if included in the text.
Now go through the same procedure with each of the other sections.

*During the writing out of this first draft, concentrate on continuity
and progression and on getting the gist of what you want to say. Don't
worry about polish and expression and style; these can be acquired
later.*

Lastly, drive home your central message in a final section headed
Conclusions or *Conclusions and recommendations.* You will finish up
with a first draft, crudely written but expressing the gist of what you
want to say in a logical sequence.

The second draft

Any fool can make a complicated subject *sound* complicated but it
takes skill and judgment to express it so that it sounds simple. It also
takes time and probably several rewrites, for it is in the rewrite stage
that acceptable writing becomes good. As you prune away the excess
words your ideas shine through more clearly. When the idea is not clear
on paper it probably isn't clear in your mind. Rewriting encourages
mental clarity in the the writer.

A report which has been written in a rush gives itself away. The
sentences are usually long and complicated; there are often too many
qualifications and too many negatives, and a fuzzy ambiguity blurs
your meaning. Continuous editing and rewriting is the only sure way to
avoid these effects; and editing your own work is not easy, for it
requires an ability to criticise yourself, to see your own work
objectively, warts and all.

After completing the first draft allow a cooling off period of two or three days. Then read through it critically. You'll see gaps in the reasoning, clumsy sequence, overgrown sentences in need of a trim, malignant constructions requiring immediate surgery. These are the faults that you will try to put right in your second draft.

As you trim and polish the report your story will gain coherence. When writing out this second draft start each section on a new page. Use subheadings to break each section into readable units. In the lines immediately below each subheading state the main point of the passage that follows. This is an important signposting technique which helps the busy executive to grasp the main points quickly – well enough, anyway, to talk intelligently about the report in meetings or discussions.

References cover literature to which you have actually referred in the text or from which you have quoted. When there are one or two references only, include these as footnotes on the appropriate page. If there are many references add a reference list at the end of the text and before the appendixes.

When you finish the second draft put it on one side for a day or two. This is an incubation period for new ideas and it will enable you to see any remaining flaws more objectively. After this time lapse check

· That you have not included any irrelevant information;
· That your style is crisp and clear;
· That you have avoided approximations ('a large number of', 'at a very high temperature'), and given precise measurements and weights;
· That your conclusions are clear and unambiguous; that any benefits to the company have been heavily stressed; and that any financial implications have been examined fully if the report has been called for by a senior manager.

The summary

After completing and correcting the second draft, write a brief summary and insert this at the beginning of the report. The summary should briefly indicate (*a*) *the purpose* of the report, (*b*) *the ground covered* by your investigation, and (*c*) your *main conclusions and recommendations*. The summary gives the substance of the report in a nutshell, focuses your reader's interest, and highlights the main conclusions and recommendations. The summary is particularly helpful to the busy executive who wants to know quickly what the report is all about and whether or not he should read it.

Now that the report is complete, draw up the final list of contents which might look something like this:

CONTENTS

Finally, have the corrected second draft typed out, duplicated and distributed.

Presenting the report

Ideally, your report should act as a lead-in to a personal presentation, so don't simply hand it in and leave it at that. To rely on the written word alone is to invite the readers to reject your proposals. There are bound to be points that you have not explained clearly, arguments the reader has misunderstood, questions you have left unanswered. Your boss may be the one to take the initiative and suggest a meeting or personal interview, but if not, take the initiative yourself: suggest a meeting is called so that you can explain and amplify your proposals and answer questions.

A face-to-face discussion is your opportunity to sell your ideas and to hammer home your main recommendations.

If you are required to 'present' your report to a committee, remember that the members are looking at you as much as at your report, trying to assess how much faith they can put in your proposals from the manner in which you present them. So be polite, dress conservatively. Point out the advantage to the members and to their departments of implementing your proposals. Angle your presentation to their point of view. When you think in terms of other people's hopes and interests they like you.

The use that will be made of your report is now out of your hands, and depends partly on the company's system of coding and classification and partly on the company's circulation lists. If both of these are adequate, you can assume that your report will be permanently and easily retrievable for use in the future, and that it will be sent to people such as planners and decision-makers, who can make use of it. If this is not the case you may need to monitor its progress and do some gentle pushing to ensure that is is seen by the right people at the right time.

A checklist for your report

1. Am I completely clear about the readership and the purpose for which the report is intended?
2. Have I drawn up a distribution list to ensure that all interested parties receive a copy?
3. Does the summary briefly but adequately explain (*a*) the purpose, (*b*) the ground covered by my investigation, and (*c*) the main conclusions and recommendations?
4. Have I made enough use of graphical aids – which have the advantage of being able to compress a mass of information into a small area?
5. Do typing, layout and design aid readability?
6. Is the language pitched at the right level for the reader? Have I avoided all unnecessary jargon? Have I defined unavoidable technical terms?
7. Have I used appendixes for facts and statistics which, if included in the text, would slow down reading and spoil the clarity?
8. Have I given the reader all the information he requires? Is all the information completely relevant?
9. Have I reached clear conclusions? Are my recommendations unambiguous, and supported by sound reasoning and by evidence about any financial implications?
10. Have I used CAPITALS for section headings and Upper and Lower Case for subheadings? Have I started each section on a new page?
11. Have I arranged the titlepage in an acceptable way or in the form preferred by the company?
12. Have I requested a face-to-face discussion for amplifying my proposals?

8 Company Publications

'A band of bewildered foremen marched on the Personnel Office.'

A company's publications are its display window round which employees and the community gather. The goods displayed there can, if tastefully arranged, tell an eloquent tale about the company's efficiency and reliability. That's why it pays to take pains over the editing and production chores. Provided these are tackled in the right way your publications can be made to work hard for you and to pay for themselves several times over.

Publishing important policies and regulations eliminates much uncertainty in the organisation. Many industrial disputes are based on speculation and misunderstanding: how many could be avoided if more companies published prompt and accurate information about their plans and policies?

When the Industrial, Educational and Research Foundation questioned nearly 800 directors about their feelings regarding business malpractices, the most common causes for concern were bribery, using confidential information for personal gain, attracting competitors' staff to gain technical information, and racial or political discrimination. Sixty per cent of the directors felt that clear rules were needed to steer managers round some of the dangers. The Poulson bankruptcy hearing with its revelations of widespread corruption in high places brings out the need for similar guidance in government and local government departments. Publishing such codes would provide clear guidelines for action.

People feel secure when the rules, the facts and the promises are in print. That is why company publications of the kind listed below can contribute to good industrial relations:

· *Company policy document* with facts about working conditions, plans, prospects, orders, personnel policy etc. Distribution: all personnel.

· *Employees' handbook* with information about the pension scheme, training opportunities, sickness benefits etc. Distribution: all employees.

· *Special management bulletins* to get urgent information to managers in advance of general announcements. Distribution: all managers and supervisors.

· *Works rules* published after agreement by both sides, with information about disputes and appeals procedure, the legislative procedure, and so on. Distribution: all managers and supervisors; all shop stewards; all notice boards.

· *Supervisors' handbook* with up-to-date information about wages, discipline, grievance procedure, safety procedures, etc. Distribution: all supervisors, foremen and charge-hands.

· *Chairman's Report to Employees*: a specially edited version of the company's annual report, picking out the highlights and aspects which specifically concern employees. Distribution: all employees; all customers.

Publications like these are the company's shop window around which employees and the community gather. Try to show them the goods they want to see and make sure they are attractively packaged — booklets which read and look like legal documents don't get read. But to justify production expenses company publications must be read, and this requires an informal, easy-to-read style and attractive presentation and layout. *Thus it is essential to take pains over the editing and production processes. Many readers will scan the company's publications for evidence of the firm's efficiency and reliability: the quality of the publication and the quality of the firm's products somehow become confused in their minds.*

One company issued a policy document which was written in language like this:

> Employees promoted to a higher job classification will be assigned the shift based on their effective seniority within the new classification.

A band of bewildered foremen marched on the Personnel Office, only to be held off by the same kind of jargon that had rocked them in the first place.

The straighter the talk, the plainer the facts, the more polished the presentation, the more efficiently will your publications work for you. Avoid obvious sales talk and PR guff because it gives a bad impression – and it won't be believed anyway.

Many large firms have a specialist technical writing or publications staff who produce all company publications, but in smaller firms the writing and editing chores are often farmed out to non-specialists. These chores may involve anything from compiling a short maintenance manual to planning an advertising campaign. Here is a step-by-step guide for the non-specialist who gets landed with this kind of job.

A step-by-step method of producing a publication

1. *Call a meeting*
After being briefed about the job, call a meeting of people whose help you will need – designers, draughtsmen, possible contributors, typists, and so on. Tell them all about the job – the purpose, the budget, time schedule, target audience etc. Try to decide in this meeting the kind of *style* and *format* that are required – e.g. will you need to use or avoid technical jargon? Are illustrations required and, if so, what kind? (Generally speaking, technical texts are much easier to read when presented with illustrations: when the reader can *see* how a machine works he gets the point much sooner than if he has to work it out from words alone.)

Call regular meetings from now on so that you can keep a check on progress, and so that the rest of the team are kept aware of what's happening.

2. *Decide on the printing method*

Your decision will be influenced by (*a*) how much money is available, (*b*) the number of copies required, (*c*) the nature of the target audience, and (*d*) whether or not illustrations are required. Figure 27 shows the main kinds of printing methods used in Britain.

3. *Draw up a time-schedule*

A wall-sheet showing the time schedule for the various stages and processes is an invaluable aid and makes it much easier for you to check progress. Once you've got a schedule, keep to it: delays can be expensive.

4. *Obtain copy and illustrations*

Give contributors as much notice as possible of the final date for handing in copy. After collecting all the copy, edit it and have it typed and sent for approval to the manager who gave you the job.

Obtain rough illustrations from photographers, draughtsmen, artists etc. Select those you want to use and send them for approval.

Order 'finished' illustrations and artwork. Remember to write a caption for each illustration used and pack each caption with information because captions are compulsive reading for most readers, including those who skip the text. Type out a separate list of captions and number them to correspond with the numbers of the illustrations.

5. *Print order*

Get a mock-up made showing the intended layout and send this for approval. Send the approved mock-up to the printers with as many detailed specifications as possible — sizes of blocks, type of paper, delivery date etc. — and obtain quotations. Select the most favourable quotation and place an order.

6. *Typefaces and illustrations*

Obtain sample sheets showing available typefaces from the printer and give him an idea of the faces you wish to use — that is, if you feel competent in this area. Do you realise, for instance, that Perpetua looks much better in large sizes than in smaller? If you don't have this kind of knowledge, better leave typeface decisions to the printer's design section or, better still, consult a professional typographical designer.

If very high quality illustrations are needed order a coated art paper: this is expensive but allows very fine detail to be reproduced. For most illustrations, uncoated imitation art paper is quite adequate.

7. *Check proofs*

Obtain *galley proofs* (long sheets) from the printer and check these for accuracy. Use standard proof-reading marks when correcting: a knowledge of the ten or twelve most-used marks should see you through (see Fig. 24). Try not to upset the printer's assembly when correcting – i.e. try to keep the lines intact because resetting an entire paragraph can be expensive.

Obtain *page proofs*. Correct and return them to the printer.

Obtain *specimen copies* of the publication. Send them for approval after checking that all the physical elements – typography, illustrations, paper, binding – are satisfactory. (These physical elements can make or mar the publication.)

Finally, check delivery dates and distribution arrangements.

Hints about layout

Layout has been described as the voice of the printed page. It attracts or repels the audience and so is just as important a factor as the information that the publication contains. For pleasing results, keep to the following principles:

1. Aim at a rough balance of black and white space on the double page.
2. Keep lines of type short for easy reading. It is difficult to pick up the following line if there are more than ten or twelve words to the line.
3. Use typographical 'colour' – bold and display type, italics, subheadings etc. – if this makes the page look more attractive and makes a complicated account or description easier to understand.
4. For some reason, the page looks more stable and balanced if the top margin is wider than the bottom and the outer margins wider than the inner.

The house magazine

At least 1,500 British companies publish a house magazine or newspaper. These publications range from the expensive and professional to shoestring efforts by some of the smaller firms. Some large firms recruit their magazine staff direct from Fleet Street, whereas a manager with no specialist training at all is often the editor in some of the smaller firms. Some companies hand over the complete job of

Proof corrections

Instruction	Marginal mark	Textual mark
Insert matter indicated in margin	New material followed by /	$\wedge$
Delete	♂	Strike through characters to be deleted
Transpose	trs	⌐ Between characters or words
Leave as printed	stet	. . . . . Under characters to remain
Begin a new paragraph	n.p.	[Before first word of new paragraphs
No fresh paragraph here	run on	Between paragraphs
Insert space	#	$\wedge$
Change to lower case	l.c.	Encircle characters to be altered
Change to italic	ital	___ Under characters to be altered
Change to bold type	bold	∿∿ Under characters to be altered
Change to small caps	s.c.	══ Under characters to be altered
Change to capital letters	caps	≡ Under characters to be altered
Change damaged characters	×	Encircle characters to be altered
Substitute or insert full stop	⊙	/Through character or $\wedge$ where required
Substitute or insert comma	,/	/Through character or $\wedge$ where required
Substitute or insert interrogation mark	?/	/Through character or $\wedge$ where required
Wrong fount : replace by letter of correct fount	w.f.	Encircle character to be altered

Fig. 24: *Use these symbols when correcting proofs. But remember that any corrections which involve alterations to your original copy will probably be charged for.*

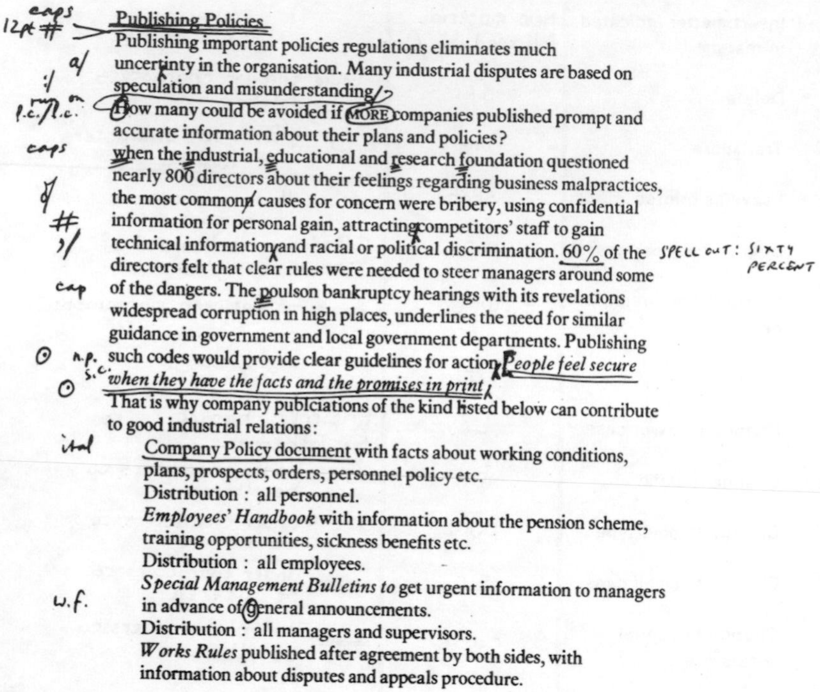

<u>Publishing Policies</u>

Publishing important policies regulations eliminates much uncertinty in the organisation. Many industrial disputes are based on speculation and misunderstanding.

How many could be avoided if MORE companies published prompt and accurate information about their plans and policies?

when the industrial, educational and research foundation questioned nearly 800 directors about their feelings regarding business malpractices, the most common causes for concern were bribery, using confidential information for personal gain, attracting competitors' staff to gain technical information and racial or political discrimination. 60% of the directors felt that clear rules were needed to steer managers around some of the dangers. The poulson bankruptcy hearings with its revelations widespread corruption in high places, underlines the need for similar guidance in government and local government departments. Publishing such codes would provide clear guidelines for action. People feel secure when they have the facts and the promises in print.

That is why company publciations of the kind listed below can contribute to good industrial relations:

Company Policy document with facts about working conditions, plans, prospects, orders, personnel policy etc.
Distribution : all personnel.
Employees' Handbook with information about the pension scheme, training opportunities, sickness benefits etc.
Distribution : all employees.
Special Management Bulletins to get urgent information to managers in advance of General announcements.
Distribution : all managers and supervisors.
Works Rules published after agreement by both sides, with information about disputes and appeals procedure.

Fig. 25: *Corrected proof.*

magazine production to one of the London firms specialising in this line.

The house journal doesn't need to be expensive and polished to make a useful contribution. Indeed, the magazine can lose its usefulness when there is too much emphasis on gloss and prestige at the expense of content. Here are some of the functions which even the homeliest journal can fulfil:

· explain the company's plans and policies and describe its range of products.
· knit together the company's many activities.
· provide a forum for grievances, controversy and ideas.

PUBLISHING POLICIES

Publishing important policies and regulations eliminates much uncertainty in the organisation. Many industrial disputes are based on speculation and misunderstanding: how many could be avoided if more companies published prompt and accurate information about their plans and policies?

When the Industrial, Educational and Research Foundation questioned nearly 800 directors about their feelings regarding business malpractices, the most common causes for concern were bribery, using confidential information for personal gain, attracting competitors' staff to gain technical information, and racial or political discrimination. Sixty per cent of the directors felt that clear rules were needed to steer managers around some of the dangers. The Poulson bankruptcy hearing with its revelations of widespread corruption in high places, underlines the need for similar guidance in government and local government departments. Publishing such codes would provide clear guidelines for action.

PEOPLE FEEL SECURE WHEN THEY HAVE THE FACTS AND THE PROMISES IN PRINT.

That is why company publications of the kind listed below can contribute to good industrial relations:

Company Policy document with facts about working conditions, plans, prospects, orders, personnel policy etc.
Distribution : all personnel.
Employees' Handbook with information about the pension scheme, training opportunities, sickness benefits etc.
Distribution : all employees.
Special Management Bulletins to get urgent information to managers in advance of general announcements.
Distribution : all managers and supervisors.
Works Rules published after agreement by both sides, with information about disputes and appeals procedure.

Fig. 26: *Final copy.*

•   allow individual employees to communicate with the entire organisation.

If you try to achieve all or several of these objectives at the same time you may fail to achieve any of them. Why not produce two publications if you wish to impress your customers *and* inform your employees? Better to aim at a single objective (perhaps this implies a single audience too) and to hit it squarely than to disperse your efforts and resources trying to hit several. This kind of dispersal only leads to weakness and failure. This is the kind of thinking that has led Wedgwood to produce three journals, each with a distinct objective and a specific target audience: a prestige news magazine for customers and shareholders; a 'parish pump' type publication for employees; and for retailers a magazine filled with product news.

As editor of the house journal you need to win the cooperation of top management so that you are kept informed of major developments in the company. And you need the support of a wide network of correspondents so that the journal has breadth and balance.

What sort of information should go into the magazine? Leading the list of employees' requests, according to one survey, is *information about company activities.* A survey conducted by *The Manager* showed that very few employees were interested 'only in information affecting me personally' and that there was wide interest in new developments, trade prospects, orders and so on. The workers, it seems, want the vital statistics rather than the usual soft chat about weddings and retirements. Regular readership surveys are probably the best way of checking that your readers are getting the kind of information they want.

Editing tips

Be very clear about the journal's objective – prestige, information, debate etc. – and avoid multiple objectives. Make sure that top management agree with this objective because you're going to need their support in achieving it. Is a magazine more appropriate than a newspaper? For instance, if your aim is to provide a news service for employees wouldn't a weekly newspaper or newsletter be better than a monthly magazine?

Try to achieve a consistent 'house style'. Be consistent about such matters as format, prose style, number of illustrations in each issue, how much paragraphs are indented, how quotations are handled (e.g. by quotation marks, indenting, smaller print etc.), kinds of typefaces used, and so on. Use typefaces which reinforce the image you are trying to present – bold, exotic, tasteful or whatever.

Cover design is extremely important, especially for prestige publications, and it may be worth paying a good designer to produce one for you.

Are you making enough use of photographs and drawings? Would pictures with fact-filled captions tell your stories more clearly and interestingly than words alone?

When editing contributors' article, use the following procedure:

· Make any changes that are needed to bring the article into line with the journal's house style.

A glossary of printing methods

Letterpress	Printing from a raised or engraved surface. Initial type-setting costs high so only economic for runs of several thousands. Letterpress and litho are the most widely used printing processes in this country.
Rotary letterpress	Prints from curved plates. Much faster than normal letterpress and normally used for runs of over 50,000.
Offset lithography	Usually called 'litho'. Printing from a flat surface — usually a zinc plate prepared with a greasy film, the ink adhering to the greasy parts. Only economical in large runs. Litho has taken over large areas of the traditional letterpress market largely because of cost advantages.
Small offset lithography	Basically the same process as offset lithography but using simplified machines. Operators of these machines can produce a limited range of work with as little as ten weeks' training.
Photogravure	The modern equivalent of engraving. Extremely expensive unless used for very large runs of, say, half a million or more. The process involves transforming the image into dots in a metal plate. The paper lifts the ink out of these dots. Allows consistent and very high quality colour reproduction. Used extensively for production of colour magazines and catalogues.
Screen printing	Often called silk-screen printing though nylon or terylene screens are usually used. The printing screen is coated with a photo-sensitised solution and the dot image transmitted onto it. The dots thus become sensitised so that ink can be squeezed through them. Used extensively for posters, plastics, bottles, containers.
Direct image	Electric typewriter used to produce a master which is photographed to produce positives or negatives for letterpress or litho plates. Or direct printing plates can be produced by the typewriter for use on small offset machines: reports are often printed by this method.
Film setting	The use of this type-setting method is spreading rapidly in this country. A photograph of the text is produced from which litho plates can be manufactured. A very fast process: computer-assisted setters can produce 2000 characters per second.
Monotype	A process which casts single characters. Used for all types of printing, particularly high-quality display catalogues.
Slug composition	Often called 'linotype'. Casts complete lines or slugs of type. Used mainly for newspaper or textbook production. For many jobs, marginally cheaper than monotype.

Fig. 27: *Print technology is an extremely complex study and becoming increasingly sophisticated — for instance, type-setting will soon be largely computerised with systems of optical character recognition making setting speeds of perhaps 20,000 characters a second possible.*

· Add an introductory paragraph which, in two or three pithy statements, crystallises the writer's argument. Thus for the reader, the opening lines contain the essence of the article, while the rest of the article is an elaboration of this opening statement.

· If necessary, add a final paragraph which (*a*) summarises the argument, and (*b*) leads to some firm conclusions. Inexperienced writers often neglect to state their conclusions and leave the reader to work them out for himself; or state them half way through the article where they are not noticed.

· If necessary, obtain more facts, details, examples from the writer with which you can fill out the body of the article. The more hard facts it contains the more interested the readers will be.

· Finally, compress the entire message into an *interesting* headline. Allusive or implication-filled headlines can be particularly effective. 'How to improve downward communication in the organisation' was the title I gave to one article. The magazine editor wisely changed this to 'How to tell the men'.

Four ways of attracting attention to your publication

1. *Attract attention with looks*
A striking cover is probably the most important attention-getting factor. But layout and design of the text are important too. Good design attracts and bad design repels. For instance, large unbroken blocks of print are bad design because they look grey and dull and weary the reader. Small blocks of print with lots of surrounding white space are far more attractive and draw the eye. Short words, short sentences, short paragraphs and frequent subheadings all create white space. And white space is an attention-getter because it makes the inner pages of the publication look attractive and makes them easier to read.

2. *Attract attention with titles and headings*
Compose titles and headings with great care. Try to make them interesting and provocative. Even the hastiest reader glances at them. If they fail to turn him on he will probably ignore the text. Use headings and titles to entice the reader into sampling the text. Use them to explain the relevance or benefit to the reader of the message that follows.

110

One good title or heading is worth a hundred lines of supporting text: don't be too anxious to throw it away with a snap word or phrase: use as many words as you need to state your central message. This is the sort of thinking that lies behind this famous advertising headline: 'At 60 miles an hour the loudest noise in this new Rolls comes from the electric clock.'

One company published a leaflet for employees with details of its new pension scheme. The original heading was *New Pension Scheme*, but when the leaflet was reprinted this was changed to *The Company's New Pension Scheme Will Increase Employees' Retirement Pay*. The revised heading is an improvement because it gives the reader the idea that there is something in the leaflet *for him*: it entices him to sample the text.

Use the first paragraph of text to elaborate on the heading or title – to explain in more detail the relevance and benefits to the reader of the message following:

Weak (company-slanted)

NEW PENSION SCHEME
Details of a new pension scheme were agreed at a meeting attended by management and union representatives, which was held on 1 August 1973. The new scheme will come into effect on 1 July 1974. Employees will be eligible to join after 12 months' continuous employment . . .

Better (reader-slanted)

COMPANY'S NEW PENSION SCHEME WILL INCREASE
EMPLOYEES' RETIREMENT PAY
At a meeting held on 1 August 1973 your union representatives accepted proposals for a new pension scheme. The new scheme will
· INCREASE the lump sum paid to employees on retirement
· INCREASE monthly pension payments to former employees.
The scheme comes into effect on 1 July 1974. You can join after 12 months' continuous service with the company . . .

3. Simplicity attracts
Simplicity is the quality that all readers want. The simpler the message the more people it will reach: the more complex the message the more

people it will lose on the way. That's why the whole of English-speaking Africa knows that Things Go Better with Big, Big Coke – if your message is simple enough you can reach a mass audience with it.[1] So to reach a wide readership

· Keep the text as short and simple as possible. Keep redrafting, simplifying and removing unnecessary detail in each successive draft.

· Use sketches, photographs, diagrams to tell your story: they *show* the reader what the message is. They can communicate a complex message quickly and simply.

· Put the key points of your message in very plain language on the first page. If necessary, develop these points in greater detail in the body of the text. Thus everybody is satisfied: the casual reader who flicks through the first few pages of the publication and quickly grasps the central message; and the reader who wants fuller information.

4. *Signposting techniques*

'Signposting' devices help the reader to grasp the key points of a complex message, prevent him drowning in detail. They include:

· Listing, at the beginning, the main points which will be dealt with in the following pages.

· Frequent headings and subheadings. These underline the key points, clarify the development of thought.

· Stating the main point of each section in the lines immediately below the subheading. If the point is very important, set these lines in italics or bold face.

· Summarising the argument or ground covered at regular intervals. Summarise the entire publication at the end of the text.

· Specifically stating, at the end of each section, any conclusions or recommendations. Answer the reader's unspoken question, 'So what?' by telling him exactly what action you wish him to take. Don't leave him to *apply* what you have been saying to his own case, don't expect him to draw his *own* conclusions: it's very likely that he won't.

[1] Edmund Carpenter, however, has argued that the simple Coke message is packed with meaning: 'Coca-Cola is far more than a cooling drink; the consumer participates, vicariously, in an much larger experience. In Africa, in Melanesia, to drink a Coke is to participate in the American way of life.' See 'The new languages' in *Explorations in Communication*, ed. E. Carpenter and M. McLuhan, Cape 1970.

Key points

1. Company publications of the kind mentioned below can improve communication between management and shop floor, contribute to good industrial relations and provide clear guidelines for action: company policy document, Chairman's Report for employees, Works Rules, Supervisors' and Employees' Handbooks, special management bulletins.

2. Attractive layout and design, straight talk and plain facts (as opposed to PR guff) all contribute to readability. Signposting techniques help the reader to grasp the key points of a complicated message. These include:

   · listing at the beginning points to be dealt with in the following pages

   · frequent headings and subheadings

   · in the lines immediately below each subheading stating the main point being made in that section

   · summarising the text at regular intervals

   · specifically stating any conclusions and recommendations.

3. Aim at an approximate balance of black and white space on the double page. Keep lines short for easy reading. Use typographical 'colour' if this makes the page look more attractive and if it makes a complicated text easier to understand.

4. Use sketches, photographs, diagrams to tell your story. They *show* the reader what you mean. They can communicate a complicated message quickly and simply.

5. When producing a publication the following sequence of operations is useful:

   · ·call a meeting of all the people whose help you are going to need: explain the job to them

   · decide on a printing method

   · draw up a time schedule – and keep to it

   · obtain copy and rough illustrations; order 'finished' illustrations

   · place print order; consult printer about the most suitable paper and about typefaces

   · check galley proofs and page proofs

   · obtain specimen copies and check that the physical elements – paper, binding, typography – are satisfactory.

6. When editing the house journal be clear about your objective and be sure that top management agrees with it. Avoid multiple objectives.

7. The editor of the house journal needs to win the cooperation of top management so that he can keep in touch with important developments in the company. He also needs the support of a wide network of correspondents from different departments and levels so that the journal has breadth and balance.

8. To add an air of professionalism to the house journal try to achieve a consistent 'house style'. Edit contributors' articles so that they conform to it.

9. Remember that employees are more interested in reading the company's vital statistics than in soft chat about weddings and socials.

10. Make sure that the magazine cover is striking and that titles and subheadings are interesting enough to entice the reader to sample the text.

9 Skills of Oral Communication

'Gestures alone can be very eloquent.'

Good oral ability is important to managers. It helps them to sell their ideas and the company's products. And it helps them with management problems because speech is a powerful agent of persuasion and control. Several surveys show that employees prefer oral communication to other methods because they feel it is reliable and provides opportunities for clarification and feedback. Thus any manager who takes the trouble to develop his speaking skills automatically develops his managerial ability at the same time.

Notice how, when the work load builds up, the harassed executive stops writing and reaches for the telephone instead, or calls a snap conference, or walks down the corridor and talks to somebody. But managers need to be good oral communicators even outside the peak periods because speech is a powerful agent of persuasion and control – which is what management is all about. The manager's function is to guide and motivate people and in achieving this, as Drucker has pointed out, his only tool is the written or spoken word. Today's employees have to be sold not told.

In one survey of a hundred company heads, ninety-eight thought the spoken word was at least as important as the written. Several surveys indicate that employees prefer oral communication to other methods: they feel it is reliable and provides opportunities for clarification and feedback. Clearly, good oral ability is important to managers. They have to talk to colleagues, customers, committees. They have to present reports and conduct interviews. Good oral ability helps them to get their ideas accepted and enables them to pass on their specialist knowledge. Moreover, every time a manager opens his mouth he is demonstrating his ability to think and analyse. Thus any manager who takes the trouble to develop his speaking skills automatically develops his managerial ability at the same time. Good oral communication can mean a new contract or a record order. The vital role of oral communication is shown by the establishment of the business lunch as an opportunity for making decisions and clinching deals.

Important areas

In spite of the obvious importance of oral communication in business few managers are competent in all aspects of it – perhaps because of a general lack of training facilities in this country. For instance, how many of these important skills have *you* mastered?

· Knowing *when* to speak: an accurate sense of timing. In meetings, being able to time your own contributions so that they achieve maximum impact.

· Knowing when to listen: knowing how to stimulate others to speak. In meetings, ensuring that nobody is excluded by drawing the shrinkers and shirkers into the discussion.

· Knowing how to trigger off the intended response in the listener: knowing how to be 'in control of' a conversation or discussion.

· Knowing how to talk to a person in an *appropriate* way; being able to make adjustments in your speech so that the listener responds without embarrassment or awareness of difference: being able to find the appropriate 'register'. The language we normally speak may sound very strange to the MD or the girls in the typing pool – but not if we know how to meet them half way, as it were, so that speech is helping rather than hindering communication.

· Knowing how to talk to mixed groups – e.g. managers and workers, professional and technical people, old and young[1] – so that nobody feels excluded. Being able to find a 'lingua franca' that enables you to communicate with all the people in the group easily and directly.

When firms begin systematically to train their managers in oral communication skills perhaps these aspects will receive more attention than the usual, formal skills of clear enunciation, voice projection, and so on.

Finding the right 'register'

The way in which different social classes vary in their speech patterns was revealed in the 1920s in the Soviet Union. The conversations of workers, peasants and soldiers was recorded and compared with the conversations of educated people. The lower social groups tended to use more words to say the same thing. And an idea which could be compressed into five words and understood by the educated groups required ten words to be understood by the uneducated. Again, the educated used more nouns, the uneducated more verbs. A manager who is skilled in the arts of communication senses differences of this kind and, perhaps unconsciously, adjusts his own speech of the people he talks to. Thus the way he addresses a meeting of shop stewards is subtly different from the way he talks to the Rotary Club – although in both cases he is being sincere and 'himself'. In each case he automatically selects the appropriate 'register', finds the kind of expression and manner which gets his message across to the listeners without causing emotional blocks such as contempt or embarrassment. *He tunes in to the listener's wavelength by subtly, and perhaps unconsciously, adjusting his vocabulary, loudness, speed of delivery and accent. The good oral communicator is almost multi-lingual.*

But many managers lack this kind of flexibility. They meet an employee in a bar, talk to him loudly in 'old boy' terms, and feel offended when the employee freezes up. Such a manager is likely to give a simple instruction to the cleaning lady in language she doesn't understand, but because of his peremptory manner she daren't ask him to explain.

Even managers who are good speakers *are often poor communicators*

[1] At one time spoken language was changing so fast that the very young and the very old could scarcely understand each other. Even today they have problems.

*because they use the same register irrespective of context. They talk in
the pub as they do in the board room and wonder at the sudden
temperature drop. They talk to the operatives as they do to the
Chairman and complain about not getting through to them.* In one
construction firm the Personnel Officer was a very pleasant man, but he
was inflexible. He had been an infantry officer, and he talked to the
employees as if they were other ranks in the Army. Of course, what was
appropriate to one situation was completely inappropriate in another,
as he discovered when several complaints were made by employees
about the way he spoke to them. His inability to switch registers
eventually led to his being removed from the firing-line and transferred
to another department.

Thus the more a manager learns about the people he has to talk to
every day, the way they think and act and speak, the better he becomes
at oral communication. The better he gets to know people the more he
realises the need for flexibility in talking to them. Finding the
appropriate register makes good relationships easier to achieve. And
vice versa.

The personal element

Different people react to the same words in different ways. You might,
for instance, talk to the breezy extrovert like this:

> Bill, I'd like you to do a bit of detective work for me. Go round the
> department and find out what people think about the proposed
> merger — the board have asked for a report. Make sure you pin them
> down — get them to say what they mean. I don't want any polite
> grunts. Put it all into a short report and add your own assessment. I
> must have this by next week.

But try talking like this to the timid little chap at the end of the
corridor. Use exactly the same words with this man and he'll probably
suffer a nervous collapse. So with him your approach has to be
different:

> Jack, I wonder if you could do a job for me? You can take as much
> time as you need over it. I'd like to find out what people in the
> department think about the merger proposals. It's really a question
> of chatting to people and trying to find out what they really think.
> I'll send a notice round saying you'll be doing this and that I'd

appreciate their cooperation. Come and see me if there are any problems and we'll see if we can sort them out.

In each case the manager is talking about the same topic. But the employee has changed. So the manager changes too. He realises the need for flexibility of approach – the importance of varying one's words and one's manner to suit the listener. But before you can do this you need to know the listener and to be aware of his preferences and needs.

The good speaker is a good listener

Good oral communication can mean talking a lot or talking a little. A manager is invited to give a speech at an Institution dinner. Being a good oral communicator he dominates his audience, provokes them with his bold ideas, dazzles them with a bravura display of wit and verbal kinetics. But during the informal discussion that follows in the bar he becomes quiet and self-effacing. He is sensitive enough to realise that the qualities he demonstrated during the formal speech would wreck a private conversation. Strong opinions and conclusions are the public speaker's friends but ruinous gaffes in informal discussion. In a private conversation the good oral communicator is not the man who speaks brilliantly but the man who draws brilliant speech from others. Drawing other people out can best be done by realising that the one subject everyone is keenly interested in is – himself. So to draw the other man out you appeal to his self-interest (you know a firm which is looking for a man with his kind of experience and qualifications; you know somebody who would like to buy his house; you know a little place where ...); or by broaching topics in which he is particularly interested or which he is particularly qualified to talk about. Make your purpose in talking match the other man's purpose in listening. If you meet a colleague at lunch who you know is dying to hear how the meeting with the General Manager went, stimulate conversation by broaching this topic at an early stage. Establish rapport, and draw the other man out by talking about his experience and problems and the subjects that interest him.

Lord Chesterfield advised his nephew to talk often but never long in conversations; never to speak of himself; and not to drop a single word that could be construed as fishing for applause.

The skilled oral communicator encourages others to contribute their *thoughts and feelings by active listening and interested questions: knowing when to listen is just as important as knowing when to speak.* Be considerate in other ways, too. In most conversational groups there's someone who's not enjoying the occasion much. For instance, somebody may be feeling hemmed in, or at a disadvantage in some other way. And some people soon become tired of talk — perhaps because of the emotional strain of thinking and feeling with others for lengthy periods; or simply because of the clatter of people's voices. In this case it may be sensible to take the hint and move away, to bring the meeting to a close, to end the interview.

On the other hand, talk with all the barbs removed can be a pretty flaccid affair, as one American visitor discovered when visiting Britain:

> It is all form and no content. Listening to Britons dining out is like watching people play first-class tennis with imaginary balls. No awkward pauses, no sense of strain, mar the gentle continuity of the talk. It goes on and on, effortlessly spinning words and words and yet more words out of the flimsiest material: gardening; English scenery; innocuous news items; yesterday's, today's and tomorrow's weather.[1]

The importance of rapport

Good oral communication depends less on using good speech forms than on establishing rapport with the listeners. That is why, in informal discussions, it is important to avoid the following common mistakes — they destroy the rapport and so reduce your effectiveness as a comunicator:

- monopolising the conversation
- flat contradictions
- vehement opinion-giving
- talking too loudly; talking to the whole room
- talking to impress; trying to be clever
- talking *at* the other people in the group
- being verbose so that the central idea gets lost in a mass of detail.

Often listening is more important than speaking. Often the words used are less important than the fact that words are being used. Nothing

[1] See Margaret Halsey, *With Malice Towards Some* (Hamish Hamilton, 1938).

needs to be said when all is understood. Even inarticulate speech becomes good communication when it achieves contact, as with the language of lovers. Speech is something that links people and allows thoughts and feelings to flow between them. Sometimes in an interdepartmental meeting or during negotiations between the unions and management, bluff and counterbluff and secrecy dominate the proceedings, and then speech becomes an empty form and no communication takes place. This kind of breakdown occurs when rivals or enemies meet and talk in the dining room. It also happens when a general discussion becomes abstract or complex: each participant is likely to lose track of what the others are trying to say, so he simply waits for a talking opportunity. When he does talk he, in turn, is ignored by the rest. Thus when the talk becomes abstract or complex it is essential to give the people you are talking to every chance to hang on to the conversation by being as specific as possible and by giving examples of every point you make. For most people abstraction is strong and nasty medicine.

Layers of meaning

More firms should consider providing systematic training in oral communication for their executives because this is potentially the most powerful form of communication. Whenever you speak to a colleague or to an employee you are really communicating several different messages. If only a man can be trained to use these messages to reinforce each other rather than in contradiction of each other powerful effects can be achieved, as the great orators have shown.

Besides your words the listener hears your emphases, pauses, accent and intonation. And he sees your facial expressions and your gestures, postures, twitches. Gestures alone can be very eloquent. Deaf and dumb people communicate efficiently using gestures and facial expressions: deaf people untutored in official deaf and dumb language use a 'natural' sign language at an even faster rate.

The very sound of the human voice has a fascination – almost a meaning of its own – quite distinct from the words. In *Communication in Africa* Leonard Doob tells of the African who listened to BBC News every night without being able to understand a word of it. The importance of the sound of the human voice is shown by a Harvard study which showed that 80 per cent of radio audiences tended to attribute physical and temperamental traits to radio speakers on the basis of voice alone. What would be the effect on your company image if the girls on the switchboard were trained to speak gently, less briskly, and learned to rid their voices of the harsh, nasal quality by speaking from the diaphragm instead of the throat?

Few writers can achieve the same range and depth of emotion that the expert speaker can evoke with his battery of pauses, emphases, gestures. With his twisting tongue and vibrating vocal chords the speaker can express a mass of subtle nuances which evaporate as soon as the speech is written down. When speech is transcribed to paper the vitality drains out of it. Little seems to be said, the speakers seem inarticulate, sentences are left unfinished, phrases are repeated, grammar and syntax are poor.[1] Some time ago I saw a television discussion between Peregrine Worsthorne, James Baldwin and Bryan Magee. While I was watching the programme – while I could see and hear the speakers – there was a sense of rich, full communication. But transcribed to paper the discussion seems weak and inarticulate, the richness has drained away:

> *Magee*: It is not true that Negroes do not vote in the United States, the proof . . . (*interrupted*)
> *Baldwin*: . . . story I told you
> *Worsthorne*: . . . ah . . . I'm perfectly prepared to agree that in the South . . . (*interrupted*)
> *Baldwin*: . . . And I ask you to . . . (*interrupted*)
> *Worsthorne*: . . . In the south the situation is extremely difficult.

Transcribed speech seems dead because a number of essential ingredients have been removed: transcribed speech captures only the verbal content and none of the many non-verbal aspects – tone, emphasis, intonation, accent, voice-quality, and so on. Consider the variety of meanings you could inject into 'So here you are at last' by saying it in different ways. But there's only one way of writing it.

Even when speech is being used with great care – during a lecture, say, or when a solicitor is explaining the law to a client – it is very loose in structure compared with writing: about half the words used don't convey information: perhaps this redundancy is needed to wipe

---

[1] In certain circumstances, such as when the speaker is very tired or upset, these characteristics of speech become very noticeable. Freud observed that disturbed patients often stumbled in their speech, stuttered, used incorrect syntax etc.

out any ambiguity or imprecision caused by the spontaneous nature of speech. Spoken language has simpler sentence structure, more slang and colloquialisms and more contractions than written language. This is one of the reasons why good speech never makes good writing and why good writing rarely makes a good speech.

Increasing your control of speaking situations

When we speak we communicate more than we say. Tone, gesture, facial expression, pauses, emphases and many other clues combine to give clues about aspects of ourselves which we try in vain to hide, or aspects of ourselves of which we are unaware. They may directly contradict the words. When this happens the communication may go wrong, or miss the target and trigger off an unintended response, as shown here:

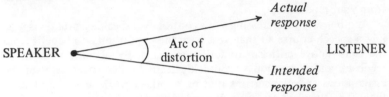

The situation slips out of your control. You must have noticed this happening sometimes when talking to colleagues, subordinates or your boss. As you talk you drift out of sympathy with each other, become secretly critical of each other, and the embarrassment builds up. You may both have been betrayed by the non-verbal aspects of your communication. Your words may be saying, 'I like you', but your posture, facial expression and gestures may be communicating contempt and distrust. To which message should the listener respond?

The study of kinesics has shown just how much information is given by 'body language', and these non-verbal aspects of speech make every sentence you utter vibrate with concentrated meaning. (McLuhan calls speech 'mental dance, non-verbal ESP'.) Edgar Schein describes how a young man reacts to an attractive girl:

> [He] will straighten his tie, pull up his socks, run his fingers through his hair, adopt a slightly more erect posture, and have a higher muscle tonus. If the girl similarly notices the young man and similarly responds to him she . . . may flush slightly, stroke her hair,

123

check her makeup, straighten her stockings, and sketchily rearrange her clothing. ... Since such clues are culturally learned, their meaning is clear to members of the same culture.

Clearly, much of the communication between boy and girl is outside of their control: they are given away by the non-verbal aspects of communication. And this is no bad thing. But when there is a similar lack of control in a business conference or in an interview the results can be disastrous.

The easiest and quickest way of becoming aware of what you are giving away is to practise speaking in a wide variety of simulated situations using a video-taperecorder. Playback instantly focuses your attention on many give-aways of which you were completely unaware. Imagine the horror of the manager who discovered that he smiled nervously and blinked rapidly every time he mentioned his boss. Once you become aware of traits like these you can usually remove them from your repertoire.

Another way of increasing your control over speaking situations is to join a speech course so that you have the opportunity to benefit from the constructive criticism of fellow students. By opening yourself to feedback and correction you quickly learn to eliminate many of the assumptions and mannerisms that make others bristle when you talk to them. The eye can't see itself. It needs a mirror.

Reminders

1. Managers need to be good oral communicators because speech is a powerful agent of persuasion and control – and that is what management is all about.
2. Several surveys show that employees prefer oral methods of communication to other methods: they feel it is reliable and provides opportunities for feedback and clarification.
3. Knowing when to listen may be as important as knowing when to speak. The ability to stimulate others to speak during discussions is as important as the ability to time one's own contributions for maximum effect.
4. In a sense, the good oral communicator is multilingual. He tunes in to the listener's wavelength and adjusts vocabulary, speed of delivery, loudness and other aspects so as to meet the other man halfway and overcome emotional blocks.

5. Strong opinions and conclusions are the public speaker's friends but ruinous gaffes in informal discussion. In private conversation the good oral communicator is not the brilliant speaker but the man who knows how to draw brilliant speech from others.

6. In informal discussion try to draw the other man out by active listening and interested questions; and by talking about his experience and problems and the subjects which he's particularly qualified to talk about.

7. In private discussion the following common mistakes destroy the rapport:
   * monopolising the conversation
   * flat contradiction
   * vehement opinion-giving
   * talking too loudly
   * talking to impress

8. The non-verbal aspects of your speech — gestures, facial expressions, posture, pauses, intonation etc. — give the listener as much information about your thoughts and feelings as your words do. Learn to control these non-verbal aspects by studying yourself on videotape.

9. People react strongly to the very sound of the human voice. For instance, people attribute physical and temperamental traits to radio speakers on the basis of voice alone. How do people respond to *your* voice over the telephone? Would you be doing the company a good turn if you arranged voice training for your telephonists?

10. When the talk becomes complex or abstract other people quickly lose track of what you are saying unless you are as specific as possible and give *concrete examples* of every generalisation.

10 Public Speakers Don't Have to be Dull

'The way to the small audience's heart is through informality.'

Every manager should be able to stand up in public and state his case effectively. It sounds a simple thing to do but how many managers can do it? Some fail to impress as public speakers because they have not realised that the craft of writing for speech is very different from the craft of writing for publication. Others fail because they are inflexible and use exactly the same approach with all audiences, not realising, for instance, that large audiences and small audiences need handling in completely different ways.

Some have great speaking ability thrust upon them. When Wesley spoke there was often mass weeping and trembling, physical collapse and protracted states of coma. Whitfield could move an audience to tears of joy simply by saying 'Mesopotamia' in different ways. Hitler could rouse a huge crowd to a frenzy. Few managers would aspire to these oratorical heights, but surely every manager should be able to stand up in public and state his case with clarity and precision. It sounds a simple thing to do but how many managers can do it? Many can't utter a dozen words in public without fretting and fuming. It's been said that a man's brain starts working before he's born and only stops when he stands up to make a speech.

Many speeches founder because although excellent as pieces of writing they sound all wrong when uttered. A good speech rarely makes good reading. That is why writing a speech calls for special art and craft. Here are some of the techniques to observe when writing the next speech you are to give to the Rotary Club or Chamber of Commerce.

Techniques for preparation of speeches

1. *Keep the speech short.* BBC further education experiments indicate that listeners' retention drops severely after fifteen minutes' straight talk and reaches saturation point after thirty minutes. It might be helpful if you wrote in a sentence at the beginning of the speech to the effect that you intend to keep the speech short to allow more time for questions afterwards. In any case, most speakers are more interesting when answering questions than when lecturing.

Because of this time factor there will be no time for elaborate introductions or other formalities so keep these elements out of the speech. To save time, make abrupt transitions from one topic to another. The audience won't mind. They are used to abrupt transitions on television news and current affairs programmes.

2. *Place strong material at the beginning of the speech.* The most important and interesting points should be made early in the speech because audiences soon flag. The material they hear while they are still alert makes the greatest impact and is best remembered. For the same reason, get to the point fast. A long build-up kills interest. It would be a pity to waste those first early, receptive minutes.

3. *Limit the speech to four or five main points; repeat them at least once.* The listener finds it harder than the reader to take in a complex message because he can't pause, go back, reread, reach for the dictionary. And he gets no help from headlines, subheadings and typographical devices such as italics or bold typeface. Thus a speech must be simple and the structure must be clear. Help the audience by keeping sentence structure simple and uninvolved, short sentences with a straightforward subject—predicate structure are the safest. Remember that even a sophisticated audience prefers the mental pampering of simple phrasing and vocabulary. Repeat your main points at the end of

127

the speech so that the audience will go away with a clear idea of your basic message.

4. *Use signposting techniques.* Begin the speech by briefly stating the points you will be dealing with: 'First I shall examine the Government's policy in this field; then deal with . . . and finally . . .' This device will help the audience to follow your argument and to see the structure of your speech. It also motivates them to listen by breaking the mental journey into short and easy stages.

5. *Make the speech looser and gentler-paced than you would if writing for publication.* Most good speeches look loose and repetitive when transcribed to paper. Published language is usually tight and compressed and highly organised. When spoken aloud it creates comprehension problems for the listener, who can't ponder and reread. So make a few points only and take your time in making them.

On the other hand, keep to the rules of good writing rather than to the rules of writing for speech if you are hoping that your speech will be reported in the Press. The relative compression and complexity may well baffle the audience but it will make impressive reading in the next day's papers. To reach a wider audience with your speech send advance copies to the Press and local radio and television stations with brief notes on the speaker and the occasion. Send copies to colleagues and business associates.

6. *State the opposing point of view.* A heavily biased, one-sided presentation will be well received only if the audience is unsophisticated and unlikely to meet with later counterarguments. Even the political parties are getting wind of this fact and the tub-thumper has disappeared from party political broadcasts. A two-sided or all-round presentation is the best tactic when dealing with a controversial subject. Such an approach is preferred by most audiences since it implies honesty and objectivity. If you present the opposing point of view sensibly, it need not damage your case. For instance, your statement of the opposition case could consist of minor points, with which the audience is already familiar, thrown into the middle of your speech — where recall is low. But there is little to be lost even from a more forceful presentation of the opposition case: presenting the other side's position somehow immunises people against subsequent exposure to it.

7. *Begin with opinions with which the audience will agree.* This increases the audience's confidence in the speaker so that they listen with more respect to the rest of his speech, including the parts which counter their own opinions (Weiss, 1957).

8. *Finally, make sure the speech will sound right.* Practise saying it aloud and listen to the results on tape. Are there too many s's or b's clustered together? Are there any awkward-sounding phrases or word combinations? Do you sound enthusiastic and interesting? Are there too many ums and ers and 'I means'? If so, you could eliminate most of these by slowing down and speaking more deliberately.

Prepare for impact

A talk is only as good as the preparation that goes into it. The more carefully you plan and prepare your speech, the more natural and interesting it will sound.

Consider your audience
Begin by finding out everything you can about the audience — how big it will be, how sophisticated and knowledgeable, its likes and dislikes. Knowing this, you will be able to talk to the audience on *their* terms and in the kind of language they prefer.

Collect your material
Collect material for your speech

· by jotting down all ideas on the subject that come into your mind
· by going to specialists and spokesmen for information
· by selective reading
· by studying any published speeches on the topic.

When you have collected more material than you can use, prune and make a final selection of interesting and relevant points.

Write out the speech in full
Write and rewrite until it comes alive and flows smoothly. Observe the rules of writing for speech which have already been discussed. Give concrete examples of every general point because these add body to the speech. Try to anticipate and answer the audience's unspoken questions. Carefully revise. Add a point here, delete a point there, clarify and polish. Has the speech got a clear structure? This is very important. Without it the audience will have great difficulty in grasping the overall

argument. Unlike the reader, the listener can't pause to unravel a point he didn't quite understand. The key to clear structure is logical progression leading to clear conclusions.

Reduce the written-out speech to numbered notes.
These will give you the key points one by one, each standing out clearly. After all the preparation, a single word or phrase will be enough to trigger off a whole string of associated ideas.

Finally, rehearse the speech
Don't read from a script or try to memorise your speech because it will sound flat and insincere, and it is the illusion of spontaneity that grips an audience. Use your numbered notes as a guide and find the actual words as you go along. Practise saying the speech in private; listen to yourself on tape to help with pace and diction. If it's not practicable to rehearse aloud, go through the speech quietly building mental sentences from the phrases in your notes.

Large audiences

A large audience has to be passive and it quickly becomes restless unless it is kept entertained. Communication has to be one-way – you to them. Encouraging participation is to invite two or three loud-mouths to steal or wreck the show. To compensate for the lack of participation you have to be interesting. A speech doesn't have to be dull if you keep to the following principles:

•   Rehearse the speech thoroughly so that a polished performance is assured.
•   Spread colour across your subject by using demonstrations and visual aids: the audience's comprehension and interest soar when they see as well as hear the message.
•   Show how what you are saying is relevant to or will benefit the listeners: 'If you introduced the following method of cost control you could reduce overheads by as much as 15 per cent.'
•   Adjust your speaking speed to suit the audience's reactions. Generally, when speaking to large groups, a disciplined delivery with careful diction and frequent pauses is necessary. Common words, short sentences and several repetitions of the central message all aid communication.

If using a microphone, don't shout into it or stare at it — both common faults. Stand at the right distance from it (usually one to two feet, though a prior trial is wise). Remember that weaving and swaying in front of the mike creates weird acoustical effects. Some microphones are very sensitive to coughs, breathing and being handled. And all microphones distort p, sh and ch sounds. A careless speaker sounds like a baby avalanche.

Antony Jay has summed up the tactics for dealing with large audiences:

> With large audiences you need maximum performing skill as a speaker, maximum slickness with visual aids and stage management, and minimum questions whereas with small audiences you need maximum question and answer, maximum informality of order and content, maximum knowledge of your subject and minimum skill as a speaker and manipulator of visual aids.[1]

The way to the small audience's heart is through informality and participation. People in a small group like to feel involved *through discussion and question and answer. A glossy presentation and slick delivery are essential when speaking to a large group but only irritate a smaller audience.*

Jitters

When the speaker is confident or appears to be confident the audience, by reflection, feel a heightened confidence in what he says. And it is remarkably easy to deceive an audience. Even when you are a bag of nerves it is easy to disguise the fact by adopting an erect posture, a steady gaze and a deliberately clear voice. Diffidence and nervousness don't matter provided they are not communicated.

The jitters are perfectly normal — even very experienced speakers get them. But after a few minutes on your feet they usually go away and you start to enjoy the experience. Nerves can raise or ruin your performance — it all depends on how well you control them. A good opening tactic is to drain some of the tension out of the atmosphere by cracking a joke or telling an amusing anecdote. Another way of controlling nerves is to use plenty of 'business' — take out a handker-

---

[1] Jay; *Effective Presentation*, p. 71.

chief, fold it carefully, tuck it in your breast pocket — while waiting for the inner turmoil to subside.

Even if your nerves do show and you start to stutter and stumble, don't worry too much. Every person in the audience is used to stuttering and stumbling in ordinary conversation and probably won't even notice your own slips. They may even *like* them. When the first man on the moon stepped out of the landing module he said he was taking a small step for man and a large step for mankind. This was clearly a stumble — probably he meant to say he was taking a small step for himself but a large step for mankind. But we all hailed it as supreme wisdom.

Next time you feel the jitters before giving a speech think of the man who had just started speaking when a concealed loudspeaker began to relay a rival's speech. Now that man had something to be nervous *about*.

Self-help

You can quickly develop your skills as a speaker by joining a public speaking course where you will be able to experiment with new methods, practise speaking in a wide range of situations, and benefit from feedback provided by the other students. If there is no suitable course available locally why not help yourself by practising with a tape recorder? It will probably draw your attention to the kind of speech faults which it is easy enough to notice in others but to which we are usually blind in ourselves: common faults are a nasal tone, fading at the ends of sentences, speaking too fast and poor articulation.

Closed circuit television is an invaluable aid for alerting speakers to poor posture, annoying mannerisms and so on.

You can also learn a lot by studying the professional speakers on television. You will notice that they use certain techniques and approaches time and time again to add impact to their words. Make a note of these techniques, and think of situations in which you might practise using them yourself.

Key points

1. When writing the speech use signposting techniques — e.g. listing at the beginning the main points to be covered. This makes it easier for the audience to follow your argument and breaks the mental journey into short and easy stages.

2. Place strong material – your most important and interesting points – near the beginning of the speech: audiences soon flag and the material they hear while still alert makes the greatest impact.
3. Keep to the rules of good writing rather than the rules of writing for speech if you are hoping that the speech will be reported by the Press: the resulting compression may baffle the audience but it will make good reading.
4. Sophisticated audiences prefer a two-sided or all-round presentation to a heavily biased, tub-thumping approach.
5. When writing your speech, collect more material than you need and prune. Write out the speech in full from this final selection of material, then reduce this draft to numbered notes.
6. With large audiences the communication has to be one-way – you to them. Since participation is ruled out they have to be kept *entertained*, otherwise they quickly become restless. So rehearse the speech carefully to assure a polished performance and use visual aids, demonstrations etc. to add interest.
7. Small audiences enjoy participating through discussion and question and answer. Thus an informal and flexible approach by the speaker is necessary.
8. To control stage fright
   · indulge in stage 'business' while waiting for the nerves to subside;
   · try to drain some of the tension out of the atmosphere with a joke or anecdote;
   · adopt an erect posture, steady gaze and deliberately clear voice – most audiences are fooled by appearances.

11 Talking to Foreigners
Some tips for the manager abroad*

'Many British businessmen are completely inexperienced in dealing with foreigners.'

Many traps lie waiting for the businessman abroad. Simple slips of grammar or vocabulary may lead to serious misunderstandings. The use of technical terms may be unavoidable, yet they can create serious difficulties of translation and comprehension. (What is the Romanian for 'dispacs' or 'parallel modes'?) The negotiator's non-verbal communication may contradict his verbal message and so prompt the other side to call his bluff. The interpreter may have difficulty in coping because of the emotional pressures of a stormy meeting. These are just some of the pitfalls. Some of the techniques for avoiding them are described here.*

Errors in grammar, syntax and vocabulary

A German businessman is telling an English sales director about an international conference he recently attended. He says that if the

* This chapter has been contributed by Dr J..Schermer.

Englishman had been there he could have made a most valuable contribution — he even suggests some subjects which he might have covered. The Englishman accepts the compliment then changes the subject and gets down to business. But something has gone wrong. The German behaves strangely, as if he's been affronted, and breaks off the interview soon afterwards. Later it emerges that the communication breakdown was caused by a simple grammatical slip. The German had used the past tense thinking that this was the correct grammatical form for the future. The conference had not yet taken place and the German was extending an invitation not expressing a compliment.

Many traps like this lie waiting for the businessman abroad. Simple slips of grammar, syntax and vocabulary can completely mislead the unwary, even lead to the collapse of negotiations. Some managers learn how to avoid these dangers from experience and appropriate training. But many British businessmen are totally *inexperienced* in dealing with foreigners; and most have received little or no formal training in the techniques of international negotiation. Yet in future years they will need to spend more and more of their time dealing with foreign businessmen because of the Common Market, the spread of multinational companies and the growth of international trade. Some of the techniques they will need to acquire are described in the following pages.

Record agreements

One of the most essential of these techniques is to put down on paper, as soon after the meeting as possible, any decisions or agreements that you think were reached during the meeting. This memorandum should then be sent to the other side for confirmation. This procedure is important because

•   any misunderstandings stemming from faulty grammar, syntax or vocabulary (as in the Anglo-German encounter described above) can quickly be cleared up;
•   it enables you to check that your own interpretation of what was accomplished in the meeting matches the assessment made by the other side;
•   it puts pressure on the other side not to change its bargaining position or to break any agreements before the next meeting.

Avoid jargon

Another important principle to observe when communicating with foreigners is to avoid the use of technical jargon as much as possible. Usually when a British manager talks business with a foreign counterpart he finds himself using two kinds of language, general and technical. By 'general' I mean the common stock of the language which everybody uses and understands. This is relatively easy to translate and easy to comprehend. But technical language, the language of the negotiator's special field of concrete technology, engineering, computers etc., can create formidable communication problems. What is the precise equivalent in Romanian for 'dispacs', 'matrices' and 'parallel modes'?

In certain exceptional cases the use of jargon can actually aid communication between foreigners for certain occupations have acquired internationally understood vocabularies of jargon words – the technical equivalents of 'bar' and 'sandwich'. By using these jargon words, nuclear physicists or colour chemists from almost any two countries may be able to talk shop more efficiently.

But most jargon lacks this kind of universal validity. And usually the danger is that when a lot of technical jargon is being tossed to and fro across the table the negotiators will fail to understand each other precisely and fully even when they themselves are unaware of this loss of focus.

The moral is to avoid technical jargon as much as possible (except in special cases) or where it can't be avoided, to ensure that a translator is hired who is knowledgeable in the subject of the discussions. Even if you can acquire the services of such a man it would be wise to take a number of further precautions. For even if the interpreter has done his homework for the occasion he may be overworked at the time; or he may have been switched from another assignment only hours or minutes before. So do some preparatory work before the meeting begins. Make sure by checking with the dictionary that he will translate accurately the key technical terms. Then, in a tactful way, ask the interpreter to describe how he understands these key concepts. If necessary, get him to list the properties and qualities he thinks they cover.

The advantages of using professional interpreters

At the same time as you are checking the interpreter's knowledge of the subject to be discussed why not make a point of finding out if he is a professional or a part-time interpreter? The part-timer (perhaps a language teacher earning pin-money) sometimes experiences difficulties in catching the precise tone and nuance of a speaker's contribution when locked in the cut-and-thrust of a bargaining battle. The communication aspect – the bluffs and counterbluffs, the ambiguous blending of cooperative phrases with those of hard intransigence, the threats to break off negotiations – all of this can create tension and confusion in an interpreter who has little experience of bargaining behaviour in his ordinary job, and the result may be that the quality of his translation is impaired. However, the professional interpreter is inured to the rough words and ways of even the hardest-boiled negotiators.

Another good reason for using the services of professional interpreters whenever possible is that they can cope with bigger 'chunks' of translation than part-timers. This improves the flow of communication because it means that the negotiators can talk for as long as they like before pausing for translation. Professionals can cope with long passages because they translate from shorthand notes, but part-timers usually play it by ear so that unless the speaker pauses for translation every two or three sentences the translation is bound to be inaccurate and incomplete.

The same effect of memory-fade explains why interrupting the interpreter in the middle of a passage of translation should be avoided: by the time he resumes his interrupted translation the message in his mind may already have lost sharpness and clarity. So no matter how badly you want to interject with a comment or question, control yourself and make a note instead and have your say only when the interpreter has stopped talking.

Bridging the cultural gap

Consider the ways in which people from different cultures express themselves. Nodding the head may mean refusal not consent. An erect posture may indicate fatigue not alertness. The foreigner may say something which, in terms of his own culture, is merely a kind word or a polite social noise but which you, in terms of your own culture, interpret as a definite promise or commitment.

When businessmen from different countries meet, cultural differences can create much misunderstanding and confusion. For instance, you can never assume that the gestures, facial expressions or even the words used by the foreigner at the other side of the table mean what you assume they mean. Equally, your own gestures, facial expressions and some of your words are just as likely to be misunderstood. The only sure way in which the negotiators concerned can bridge this particular communication gap is by firsthand experience of each other's country.

This explains why a company's training programme for its international negotiators ought, perhaps, to be set in one or several foreign capitals. But this is the long-term solution. One short-term answer to the problem is to use the interpreter as a kind of cross-cultural guide.

A professional interpreter would never volunteer his own comments and explanations of the passage he was translating. He would regard such additions almost as a kind of unprofessional conduct, and see his first duty as being to translate, adding nothing and leaving nothing out. But when his role is limited to translation his special knowledge of the other side's feelings and reactions remains completely untapped.

The interpreter either belongs to the same culture as the foreign businessmen you are talking to or, in the course of his training, he has acquired firsthand experience of it. So he is probably a far more accurate judge than you are of what the other side is really thinking and feeling behind its façade of words. His firsthand experience of their culture enables him to read their body language – the language of face, eyes, posture and gesture – which are often more reliable indicators of feeling than are words alone. He *knows* that a smile at this point indicates disappointment. He *senses* that a display of enthusiasm at that point is really a polite way of expressing angry rejection. And so on.

So at the start of the proceedings why not invite the interpreter to use his own initiative and give you – alongside his translations – a kind of running commentary on the other side's reactions? ('He's smiling, but that only shows how angry he is'; 'I don't think he means you to take that last proposal seriously' etc.) The extra information you gain by this procedure can strengthen your bargaining position and enable you to make necessary tactical changes. And it will allow you to bridge some of the numerous communication gaps caused by cultural differences.

Feedback signals

Here is another useful device for boosting the accuracy of your communication in encounters with foreign businessmen.

If, while talking in a meeting, you make a point of looking at the interpreter rather than at your opposite number you will receive a stream of feedback signals from his face, eyes and body which will tell you whether you are talking too fast or too slow, whether you are making your meaning plain, whether the terms of an offer are too hard or too soft, and so on. Deliberately looking for clues of this kind — deliberately opening yourself to feedback — helps you to keep your communication on-target and elicit the response you intended from the other side:

Negotiator: If you would agree to this we would then be prepared to
lend you the required sum at an interest rate of 10 per
cent *[At this point the interpreter glances up with
surprise: clearly, 10 per cent strikes him as rather steep.
This is what you'd suspected yourself, and now you are
sure. So you go on:]* I was going to suggest a 10 per cent
interest charge, but I think that possibly we could reduce
this slightly although I shall have to get instructions from
head office first.

Remember that you are yourself involuntarily sending out a stream of signals which communicate feelings and thoughts which you'd prefer to keep to yourself. The danger is that your non-verbal message will contradict your verbal one, perhaps undermining your bargaining position or prompting the other side to call your bluff.

Thus it is extremely important for the negotiator to develop his self-awareness and self-control so that, in effect, he never gives himself away. In developing this kind of self-control a video-taperecorder is an invaluable training aid. It enables the trainee to see for himself, after mock encounters, the ways in which his words belie the language of his face, hands and body.

Removing uncertainty

Imagine that the businessman opposite you is talking in his own language. You don't understand the words he is using but you do get some impression of his meaning from his posture, facial expression and gestures. He pauses, and now the interpreter translates what has just been said. But the translation completely contradicts the impression you gained. Clearly it is important to remove the uncertainty as soon as possible, otherwise you risk irritating frustration and delays later in the session, or even a communication breakdown.

When uncertainty of this kind crops up the simplest way of dealing with it is to take the interpreter aside during the next tea break and clarify the passage with him. It may turn out that he has misunderstood or misinterpreted the point, or that he has unintentionally put the emphasis in the wrong place. If necessary, the point can be taken up with the other side immediately afterwards.

Much gratuitous uncertainty can be created when confidential matters are discussed between members of the team in the interpreter's presence. When this happens the interpreter usually wonders if he is expected to pass on what he has learned to the other side; you in turn wonder exactly how much of what was said has been passed on and what the other side made of it. *So unless you enjoy working in an atmosphere of ambiguity and uncertainty don't discuss confidential matters when the interpreter is around. Be particularly discreet when he is employed by the other side, for it may be that his professional code of impartiality will clash with his patriotic or organisational code of loyalty. In other words, he may give the game away.*

Many traps lie waiting for the British manager who has to negotiate with foreigners. Misunderstandings easily occur, communication breakdowns are easily caused. Fortunately, though, it is possible to avoid some of the dangers by learning a few simple techniques such as those described in this chapter, then practising them at every opportunity until they become second nature. Once this has happened, talking with foreigners should become a less embarrass'ng and more rewarding exercise.

Summary

1. As soon after the meeting as possible, put down on paper any decisions or agreements that were reached then send this memorandum to the other side for confirmation. Thus any misunderstandings can quickly be cleared up, and the other side is also encouraged not to change its bargaining position before the next meeting.
2. Generally, avoid the use of technical jargon in meetings with foreigners. It causes problems both of translation and comprehension.

3. Where you anticipate having to use a lot of technical language in a meeting, try to acquire the services of an interpreter who is knowledgeable in the subject to be discussed. As a further safeguard, check with him, before the meeting begins, that he has a precise understanding of the key technical terms that you are going to use.
4. Remember that professional interpreters can usually cope with bigger 'chunks' of translation than part-timers. Remember, too, that part-time interpreters are not as inured as professionals to the rough words and ways of some negotiators, and that during rowdy sessions the quality of their translations may be impaired as a result.
5. The interpreter is probably a better judge than you are of what the other side is really thinking and feeling behind its façade of words. So why not invite him to give you, alongside his translations, a kind of running commentary on the other side's reactions?
6. An international negotiator has to develop his self-awareness and self-control so that, in effect, he doesn't give himself away in meetings. The use of a video-taperecorder in training sessions enables him to see for himself the ways in which his 'body language' contradicts his words.

12 Listen, Managers!

'Poor listening can damage the organisation.'

In most companies listening carries a large part of the total communication burden. Yet some managers strangle communication because they can't or won't listen properly. The higher a manager climbs the more he needs good listening because of more meetings, more interviews, more decision-making. Some of the techniques for developing good listening habits are outlined in this chapter.

An engineering firm which, in previous years, had met union officials only to sort out grievances and disputes decided to ask the union to meet management regularly, reason or no reason. So once a week the two sides met — just sat and talked informally. For the first time each side found itself really listening to the other. Sensitive areas were spotted before they became explosive. Sometimes the problem disappeared into thin air as one side talked and the other side listened. When the number of disputes in the factory dropped management linked this with these informal listening sessions. Thus they soon paid for themselves many times over.

When people in commerce and industry don't listen to each other the results can be costly. Disputes flare up apparently out of nothing. Simple arrangements and straightforward agreements go wrong. How often have your own clear utterances been misinterpreted or not noted or implemented wrongly? The ear functions poorly in the business world. Yet in most companies listening carries a large part of the total communication burden. Executives spend up to 40 per cent of their time listening. Yet half of any oral message is forgotten by an untrained listener within eight hours and US Army research has shown that only one-tenth of the original message remains after three days.

Listening is sometimes written off as a merely passive skill. But it is more than that, for it is the listener who communicates rather than the speaker: unless somebody listens to the message and understands it there is no communication, only noise.

Neurotic managers?

A survey of leading industrialists by a team of researchers revealed a strong preference in the board rooms for oral methods of transmitting 'very important' policies: the preferred method was to explain the new plan or policy at a meeting of managers. Whatever people's preferences much top level communication must be done orally, and especially where speed of communication is a vital factor. For the written word is slow compared with the spoken word – and this makes listening more and more important in this age of speed. For all these reasons, listening ability is a key management skill. Yet how many managers possess it?

McGregor's Theory Y makes out a convincing case for management by listening. But one industrial psychologist, M. H. Knowles, has implied that many managers are constitutionally incapable of listening well. According to Knowles, it is the neurotic, authoritarian personality who tends to get himself promoted into managerial position. And companies are full of emotionally unstable executives who can neither express their own feelings nor listen properly to others! Other authorities (McMurry, Eliasberg etc.) argue that many managers have unconscious aggressive feelings and lust for power that drastically limit their ability to listen, say, to trade union representatives and to negotiate intelligently.

Such managers are falling down on the one technique that could tell them where they are going wrong.

Poor listening can damage the organisation. The manager who can't or won't listen to his subordinates may therefore lurch blindly from

143

one top-heavy policy to another. Listening adds breadth and validity to decision-making. And by listening to people the manager learns how to deal with them – he discovers how their minds work and their approach to problems. Moreover, the efficiency of subordinates depends partly on how well they are *listened to.* Imagine, for instance, that one of your assistants steams up to you in the corridor. He's had a grievance bubbling and boiling inside him all morning. Now he erupts. You listen patiently and sympathetically. You accept his criticisms because you can deal with the emotions they arouse in you. So the anger drains out of him. He goes away mollified. You go away a much wiser man.

Every day the manager who listens becomes wiser and wiser. For careful listening persuades people to unlock their feelings and display their true thoughts. As William Keefe[1] has said: 'The listening manager, because he listens well, has his mental stethoscope on the heartbeat of the organisation and can usually predict what changes are needed and will occur.'

To listen to the heartbeat of your own section or department you could hold small, informal get-togethers over coffee with subordinates. Many employees freeze in large meetings, look embarrassed when alone with the boss, but in small groups they come alive. The effectiveness of such encounters depends largely on the listening ability of the senior man present. Provided he's able and willing to listen properly he'll get the grapevine information he needs for decisions and policy-making. Subordinates will probably leave these coffee conferences with an increased sense of participation and wellbeing.

Why put it in writing?

Many managers, aware of their own and their colleagues' inability to listen well, prefer to 'put it in writing' instead. Much information needs to be put on record but the practice can be carried too far. The simplest arrangement is confirmed by memo or letter. Insignificant instructions or trifling details of policy are composed and typed and duplicated and circulated – and sometimes they are read. One result is information overload, that torment of senior executives. Yet when matters must be settled in a hurry the typewriters keys stop clicking and the manager reaches for the telephone instead.

[1] William F. Keefe: *Listen, Management!* (McGraw-Hill, 1971), p. 39.

Putting it in writing requires more staff, more equipment and a bigger budget than efficient listening. *So how much a year would the improved use of listening skills by its managers be worth to your firm? Measured against the savings the cost of training would surely be negligible.*

Reading	4%
Writing	11%
Speaking	22%
Listening	63%

Fig. 28: *A survey by the American Dietetic Association showing how members spend their time communicating, highlights the importance of listening in an average working day.*

Can you be communicated with?

Some managers take pride in their ever open doors. Yet their subordinates, when they go through them, feel inhibited. They can't speak freely about problems that should be discussed for the benefit of both parties. The boss fails to listen properly, and men don't talk freely to someone who doesn't listen. Result: the man withdraws, the boss rests in peace, the problem remains, the company foots the bill.

Some bosses simply can't be communicated with and the temptation is to tell such men what they want to hear, whether or not it's the whole story. The performance of both parties must suffer as a result. To be communicated with is a dangerous proposition to some people, endangering their own feelings, threatening their self-esteem; so they don't really listen, picking up the speaker on minor details, or giving him inadequate time to state his case fully.

No doubt some companies could improve communication by

145

modifying selection methods so that those appointed to positions of responsibility would stimulate upward communication because they were the sort of people they were, and because of the quality of their listening.

The higher a manager climbs the more he needs good listening because of more meetings, more interviewing and counselling, more decision-making. The higher he goes the more removed he is from the detailed activity on the firing line. Unless he can somehow encourage a strong and continuous upward flow of information the senior manager is bound to be left in the dark about what's happening on the shop floor, and he will lack sufficient accurate information on which to base sound decisions. The temptation is always to interpret no news as good news. But lack of complaints and of information about problems may only be an indication that upward communication is being blocked by somebody's deafness.

Policy-making should surely be based on the activity of the whole factory. And what better way of tapping the reactions and opinions of subordinates than by efficient listening to the many day-to-day informal contacts within the department and outside it. Only highly specific grievances can be dealt with through union channels – a new safety-guard for a machine, the rate for a particular job – which leaves the man's boss as the obvious person to go to with problems. And when the man talks he's entitled to expect his boss to listen properly. Indeed, a company without managers who know how to listen is like a man without sight and hearing, cut off from what goes on all around. Such a company functions on a reflex basis like one of the lower organisms. It lurches blindly from decision to decision, never knowing in advance the likely reactions of employees.

Deafening emotions

The ever-open door – the mere mechanics of communication – is less important than the attitudes of the men on either side of it. If there is no point of emotional contact there can be no real communication. A minimum requirement is a degree of mutual trust. After studying communication in the coal mines Revans noted that many approaches to the miners were made in trying to raise output, including a personal letter from the Prime Minister. But, Revans concluded, merely communicating does not succeed in modifying the underlying attitude of mistrust upon which credibility appears to be based. Broadly similar conclusions were reached by Mellinger, 1956, who found that lack of trust is an important factor keeping men from talking to their bosses.

The reason for many communication breakdowns in industry is that the emotions act as aural filters. Either we fail to listen to somebody we distrust or we listen *too* keenly to somebody we like. Women are easy targets for flattery, and managers, too, listen eagerly when the message is something they want to hear — the value of their own work, say — but switch off when they hear something unpleasant, such as praise of a rival. Instead of listening properly and coolly assessing the evidence we spend the time assembling an opposing case, or thinking up awkward questions, or making mental rejection noises. The filters can also change emphasis or twist things round. So unless we are trained to resist this tendency the message is maimed. And the error may be compounded, for only one bad listener is needed to stop or distort communication up or down the organisation chain.

Try to stop yourself reacting emotionally to the speaker's clothes, the length of his hair, his looks, his posture, the colour of his skin. An emotional response from you may stop you hearing an important message or a new idea. Deliberately keep your mind wide open to what he is saying. This means accepting that you may have to change as a result of what he's going to tell you. And it involves a refusal to react hastily or emotionally. A deliberate commitment of this kind will take the interior 'static' out of listening.

Training techniques

Various training techniques have been developed to counteract this kind of partial listening. During role-playing sessions, 'senior managers' listen to complaints from 'subordinates'. Afterwards, each is required to repeat the other's arguments accurately. Observers comment on how well the trainees listened to each other, whether they stopped themselves reacting emotionally, whether the senior's manner encouraged the junior to speak freely: the trainees discover that the wrong gesture or facial expression can stop the other man talking as surely as if he'd been told to go to hell. So the trainees learn not to give negative responses and to hear the speaker out; and to *reserve judgment* until later, after a cooling-off period.

When the junior shows aggression the senior learns to let him go on without interruption until the flow stops. No attempt is made to steer the speaker back onto the right track because the right track may be the wrong track. In the workplace, listening to subordinates in this way may reveal sore spots in the organisation that need corrective action.

Another way of sensitising managers to the importance of good listening in meetings is to record a training meeting on tape. The chairman forces careful listening by ruling that all speakers should have their say without interruption. Members are allowed to speak only after first restating the ideas and feelings of the previous speaker accurately. Negative emotion drains out of the discussion and differences are reduced. Not surprisingly, for members have to listen to each other so closely that they are able to make accurate summaries. The tape is later played back to the group and analysed in terms of listening.

Other useful training methods are:

1. Trainees do a listening comprehension test then discuss with the tutor the meaning of their scores.
2. Trainees are grouped in pairs. Each speaks and listens to his partner. Afterwards each evaluates the other's listening ability.
3. Trainees listen to a taped speech and then write a report on it, stating its purpose and the main ideas. Trainees exchange reports and discuss the reasons for any differences in their answers.

Practical exercises of this kind could readily be undertaken by most training departments.

Trainees whose listening ability has been sharpened through training often report that one result is an improvement in relationships between themselves and their subordinates. When employees find the intention to listen and understand, their hostile feelings towards management are reduced. Moreover, the managers themselves become less dogmatic in their ideas, more sensitive to the feelings of their subordinates.

Meetings: the dialogue of the deaf

Industrial organisation has become so complex that the executive job has outgrown the ability of a single decision-making head. The manager-hero is dead. Most modern industrial problems are really compendiums of sub-problems with different experts handling different aspects. Day by day, information is exchanged, meetings are called, and gradually the team inches its way towards the final solution: the plant

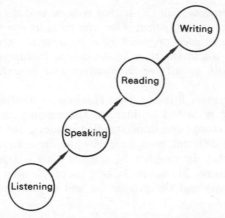

Fig. 29: *There seems to be a sequence in language growth from listening to speaking to reading and eventually to writing. Thus good listening is important to all other aspects of communication.*

is installed, the project developed, the order completed. These are the facts of life in modern industry. They explain the rapid expansion of group processes in British industry over the past two or three decades. Meetings play an important role in the modern business world.

Meetings work best when all the different viewpoints are given a fair hearing, yet often members fail to listen properly to points that don't match their own ideas.[1] Or they split into camps and, instead of listening to understand, each camp listens for weaknesses in the evidence of the other. Ideas are classified as ours or theirs, good or bad. Often all-or-nothing choices are made between contradictory proposals. People stop listening to *all* the evidence. As a result judgment becomes distorted and wrong decisions are made.

What Norman Maier describes as the 'two-column method' is a useful technique for overcoming this kind of semi-listening. Each suggested solution is dealt with in turn. First the chairman invites facts and ideas for entry in the first column, which is reserved for 'good points'. Then

---

[1] Members tend to resist listening to differing viewpoints because 'through such understanding the individual found that the opposing viewpoint had more merit than previously he would allow to emerge into consciousness ... he ran the danger of recognising that he, rather than his opponent, should change'. (George Muench, 1963).

149

'bad points' are assembled in the second column, and the two columns then weighed against each other. Thus the group is forced to make a proper evaluation of each proposal by comparing the pros and cons. The question for discussion then becomes how to capture the major advantages of both or all the alternatives and how to avoid the disadvantages.

People do far more listening than speaking in meetings. So more efficient listening is bound to increase the meeting's efficiency by facilitating the exchange and understanding of ideas. The more closely you listen to the different points of view the more accurate is your picture of just what the problem is, and the more relevant your own contributions become. Moreover, talking to people who really listen encourages creativity and the production and expression of new and better ideas.

Stop listening to yourself

While others talk the worst listeners simply collect their own thoughts for the next speaking opportunity. But even somebody who tries his best to listen properly has problems. Average talking speed, say 120 words a minute, is slow going for the human brain. Most people read faster than this (reading speeds of 600 words a minute are possible after training), and thoughts are created at faster speeds still. The result is that no matter how hard we listen it is difficult to stop the flow of our own thought. Ralph Nichols and Leonard Stevens have described in convincing detail what happens and suggested ways of dealing with the problem: as we listen we still have spare time for thinking. A kind of energy gap is created and we fill the gap with our own thoughts and words. What we hear is a kind of counterpoint – our own words and thoughts intermingled with those of the speaker.

This kind of cacophony erupts when colleagues meet to discuss a business problem or when an employee talks to his boss. As the speaker outlines his case the listener can hardly resist dashing down mental sidetracks. The time comes when, returning from a sidetrack, he jumps back into the sluggish stream of words only to find he has missed the boat. Part of the message has been lost and what is being said now doesn't make sense. So the listener leaves for another mental sortie. More and more of what the speaker is saying is lost on the listener and communication atrophies. The other man senses this and gets up to go, his problem unresolved.

Nichols and Stevens recommend a number of deliberate mental activities to overcome this effect. These include mentally summarising, from time to time, the points made by the speaker so far; anticipating where the speaker is moving and what conclusions he will draw; assessing facial expressions and gestures for meaning.

Some firms, such as the General Electric Company, have developed listening improvement programmes for executives which use these and other techniques. Many American universities and business colleges run listening courses. In this country a number of polytechnics and technical colleges run communication courses that give some attention to the subject.

Listen for the main points

Oral language tends to be discursive and loose in structure. Words are used loosely and inaccurately. Syntax and grammar are poor. Phrases are repeated and sentences left unfinished. Grunts, oh's and ah's make the speech staccato and interruptive – difficult to follow. (Harold Pinter's dialogue precisely captures these characteristics.) Usually a person begins speaking without prior formulation of his thoughts, unlike the writer, and he consequently drifts into and out of subjects with no clear beginning and end.

This creates problems for the listener. Exactly what – behind all the grunts and groans and tangled constructions – is the man saying? The problem is compounded when the speaker is a muddled sort of person anyway and doesn't organise his thoughts too well. In these cases it is extremely difficult to understand what he's talking about. And yet it's up to you, as the listener, to organise his thoughts for him in your own mind, while he's talking.

This can be done only if we remember that the ideas the speaker is trying to communicate are far more important to him than the individual phrases or the details. Thus trying to memorise or make sense of every detail is bad listening – in the same way as trying to read every word is bad reading – for the overall pattern of the statement is likely to become blurred. It is more important to see the shape of the argument than to make sense of all the details.

A colleague who stops you in the corridor and talks to you for five or ten minutes will probably make four or five main points – the unfolding of these points constitutes his 'case'. So consciously listen for these main points and look for the connections between them. Don't

151

attempt to make sense of all the details and supporting evidence. If you are unsure about what the main ideas are, ask questions which encourage him to repeat or clarify them. If you listen properly you will be able, at the end, mentally to summarise his main points together with the main supporting details.

In formal speeches the key to the structure is frequently given at the beginning of the speech and again at the end when the speaker summarises. In his opening remarks, for instance, the speaker may say something on these lines: 'I should like to remind you of the way in which this company used to handle personnel recruitment in the past; then take a critical look at present methods; and last, consider some changes that are necessary if we are to remain competitive.' Here is the key to the whole speech.

Total listening efficiency is impossible

Total listening efficiency is, of course, a pipe dream. There are simply too many obstacles, as the Rosin Engineering Company discovered after moving into new headquarters in the Midlands. The company was forced to call in a Black Country dialect expert to 'translate' the language used by local employees, which was full of words like 'chomble' (chew over), 'lommock' (make wild), and 'noggenvedded' (stupid). There are class and occupational jargons; and different generations use language differently. A person's generation is revealed by the construction of his sentences and such characteristics as rapidity (directness) or slowness (periphrases). Youthful language is elliptic, allusive, and full of unspoken implications that older people have trouble in grasping. When an older person speaks, the message can often be seen coming by a younger listener who is thus tempted to go off into a mental sidetrack.

When one investigator tried to establish what three different groups of people in industry (industrial psychologists, personnel administrators and foremen) accepted as the meaning of several words in common use – efficiency, incentive, productivity, and the like – he found that none of the words was defined in a single and uniform way. In fact, interpretation of some of the words varied greatly. Messages full of words like this are a kind of verbal rococo on whose curlicues the listener gets hooked. Yet in industry words like this are used all the time – as a glance at most notice boards will confirm. *The moral, I*

suppose, is that managers should choose their words wit[h]
them where necessary and supplying concrete examples.

Even non-oral aspects of communication throw up prob[lems for the]
listener. For instance, a facial expression or a gesture [may mean]
different things to speaker and listener. Ruesch and Ke[.....]o,
observed how British and American gestures are directed towards
activity ('Come over here'; 'That one'); Italian gestures express
emotion; Jewish gestures accompany words to underline the points
made, and so on. Different groups use different 'codes' and this can
mislead the listener.

In spite of all the obstacles, companies have much to gain from the
improved use of listening skills by their managers. At every level people
should be able to talk to their boss in the expectation of being listened
to and understood. Colleagues should be able to make simple
arrangements and agreements without feeling the need to put it in
writing and adding to the information overload. Business meetings
which divide into 'camps' and which switch off when the other side is
speaking will work inefficiently and frequently make the wrong

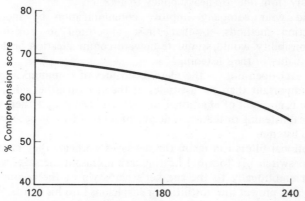

Effects of Accelerated Speech

Speed of spoken presentation of material in words per minute

Fig. 30: *Tests carried out at the North Staffordshire Polytechnic suggest that
there is only slight comprehension loss when informational material is
presented at twice normal speaking speed. If this is so there are many practical
implications. For instance, educational television and radio programmes and
films could have far more information squeezed into their commentaries.*

decisions. And unless managers and trade union officials learn to listen to each other properly distrust and hostility will remain and disputes will continue to flare up without warning. For all these reasons, many companies would gain a lot from training their managers in efficient listening, how it works and where its value lies. At the present time training opportunities in this country are very limited and companies would probably need to devise their own training schemes. But the expense would surely be justified, because companies which have introduced listening improvement programmes have found that they pay for themselves many times over.

Key points

1. In most companies listening carries a large part of the total communication burden. Executives spend up to 40 per cent of their time listening. Yet without training listeners are likely to forget half of any oral message within eight hours.

2. Good listening adds breadth and validity to decision-making. The manager who can't or won't listen to his subordinates may lurch blindly from one top-heavy policy to another.

3. Could your company improve communication by modifying selection methods so that those appointed to positions of responsibility would stimulate upward communication because of the quality of their listening?

4. The ever open door – the mere mechanics of communication – is less important than the attitudes of the men on either side of it. If there is no point of emotional contact between people there can be no real listening or telling. A degree of mutual trust is necessary for good listening.

5. Emotional filters can maim the messages we hear: they may cause us to switch off to avoid hearing an unpleasant message; we may react emotionally to the speaker's hair-style or the colour of his skin and project our hostilities or suspicions into his words. We can take much of the 'static' out of our listening by *refusing* to react hastily or emotionally.

6. The two-column method is a good way of preventing people in meetings from splitting into rival camps. This method forces the group to make a proper estimate of each proposal by comparing the pros and cons of each one in turn.

7. Trying to memorise or make sense of each detail is bad listening. It is more important to see the shape of the overall argument than to make sense of all the details. Consciously listen for the key points and the connections between them and let the minute details and supporting points glide by.

8. In a formal speech the key to the speech's structure is often contained in the speaker's opening or closing remarks: 'First I shall deal with . . . then with . . . and finally with . . .'

9. Don't allow your prejudices to be triggered off by certain buzz-words and buzz-subjects — e.g. strikes, nationalisation, 'Reds', 'permissive'. Withhold judgment until you have all the facts and any emotion has died away.

10. Good listening is active not passive: it is necessary to encourage the speaker by interested expression and questions and an alert manner. Actively listen for the non-verbal messages: 'If his words say, "Well, it really isn't very important to me anyway", but his posture is stiff, his knuckles white, his eyes hopeful and his forehead glistening with perspiration, you had better hear the nonverbal message.'[1]

---

[1] Norman Sigband: 'Listen to what you can't hear', *Nation's Business*, June 1969, p. 72.

13 The Media Message

Company media, properly used, can powerfully amplify the manager's voice

'Some subjects lend themselves to visual presentation.'

Modern media are capable of powerfully amplifying the manager's voice. Yet most managers fail to exploit them to the full because the knowhow is lacking. And even the most sophisticated equipment is only as efficient as its users. Efficient use means exploiting the media for what they are good at expressing – for instance, using mass media (such as the house magazine) to consolidate information already transmitted via line channels. Another sound principle is to use media in combinations when transmitting important messages. The people you miss with the first shot you hit with the second: both groups are then alerted for later messages.

Every member of your staff is a victim of communication overkill. Each one of them is exposed to about 1,5000 messages a day. This being the case, how can you make sure that *your* voice is heard above the din? One answer is to use company media to plough your message through the listening barriers.

Most managers are surrounded by powerful instruments which are capable of penetrating every crack and cranny in the company and of making a wide range of appeals to the minds and senses of employees. This equipment can powerfully amplify the manager's voice but often managers fail to exploit it to the full because the knowhow is lacking. Some firms spend millions on sophisticated communications equipment yet jib at spending hundreds or thousands on training people to make the most of it. And training is needed. When Purdue University researchers asked company heads what they thought was the main reason for communication breakdowns in their companies the most common answer was 'inadequate use of media'.

Communicating in the modern organisation requires special skills and training. Getting a message around a crowded office presents few problems: a hand-to-hand memo will do the job quickly and simply. But communicating with miners scattered across the coalface or with a large sales force scattered across the country presents tougher problems and requires a more sophisticated approach and, probably, the use of gadgetry. In the coal mines closed-circuit television is used to provide instantaneous and simultaneous communication with the miners. BP wanted to communicate a new pricing policy to 5,000 salesmen. So it made an inexpensive film on videotape and showed it simultaneously in twenty-two centres to all the salesmen affected, at a cost of only £1 per head.

Perhaps with the advent of electronic media we shall soon be seeing the twilight of print.

Formidable information or communication problems shrink when the right equipment is available. Think of the mass of information lying in your office at this moment waiting to be processed and used and filed. Then think of how a baby computer could store and retrieve all this information for you at the touch of a button. But even if there is a baby computer in the firm people will fail to use it unless they know which buttons to press.

Here are just a few of the media available in most large organisations which make traditional written and oral methods a dreary second- or third-best:

·   *CCTV* is used daily in the coal mines to communicate with a scattered and inaccessible work force.

·   *An internal telephone link-up* is available which allows up to ten people to talk together during snap conferences.

·   *Pocket radio-telephones* enable the manager to dial into private telephone exchanges from a distance of several miles.

·   *Facsimile transmission*, a small gadget which is clipped to the telephone, allows accurate copies of maps, documents etc. to be sent to any part of the world accurately and instantly.

· | *The GPO's Confravision service* enables businessmen to confer at long distance by providing sound and vision facilities between groups of people in studios any distance apart. The studios are private and the customers can operate the service themselves so that confidential documents can be shown with complete security. There should be a nationwide network of Contravision studios by the 1980s.

·   *At Boeing a teleprocessing system* sends immediate and simultaneous notification of arrival of goods to the accounts department, inventory control, warehouses etc. There are no delays and capital is freed which would be tied up in additional inventory if conventional written reports and memos were used.

In one big library *a colour code* leads the student to the department he needs. Once there he plugs into *an information station* for more detailed information.

·   *Electronic speaking machines* which may provide voices for computers are being developed in the United States. When computers can speak they will be able to handle many more tasks. The telephone on your desk might serve as a computer terminal and provide instant access to such things as airline and hotel reservations, inventory reports, and so on, with the information you need coming back immediately in spoken form.

Developments like these point up the crisis of conventional media and methods of communication which sometimes limp behind the new technology and the new concepts. Perhaps, indeed, communication equipment and systems are reaching the outer limits of sophistication and a single extra increment of complexity will render them useless to all except the dedicated.

Even the most sophisticated media are only as efficient as their users. Remember the story of the junior manager who sent his first telex message on the Monday, followed it up on the Tuesday with a telephone call to check that it had arrived, then wrote a memo on the Wednesday to confirm the telephone conversation.

Use media selectively

Each one of the media speaks a unique language, presents the facts in a special way. If used to complement each other the media can offer management a powerful extension of its voice and influence. Harold Mendelssohn calculated that an average person receives about 1,500 messages a day – a horrifying case of communication overkill. But by using media in an educated way you can make sure that your voice is heard above the surrounding babble. This means using the media to express what they are good at expressing. Television has different powers of expression from print, different again from radio or posters.

Use the media selectively for particular effects. Create a swift, sharp-etched impression of a person with television. Search that person's inner world with print. Report an operation on his eye with film. Change his attitudes by involving him in group discussion. Using the media least suitable for a specific purpose is expensive and time-wasting, like driving yourself to the office by tractor. One company decided to use film to give a face-lift to the company image. The film was made and free shows were run in several different locations but only a handful of people turned up – at a cost of £10 per head. Using film was an expensive mistake. Nobody on the board realised that film and the other mass media are relatively powerless to alter *opinion* or *attitude*; or that in any case there are far cheaper ways of getting a message to the public.

In a number of wartime studies Hovland and his associates found film effective in conveying factual information, much less effective in changing specific opinions and totally ineffective in changing general attitudes. Many studies since then confirm that the mass media in general cannot alter beliefs and behaviour except in trivial ways – hair style, and so on. *So don't use the company mass media to try to change employees' feelings about management. Do use them to consolidate information already transmitted through line channels.*

Use the medium most appropriate to both subject and audience.

159

Some subjects lend themselves to visual, others to verbal presentation. To explain a new plant or factory design to your employees you would use a model or drawing but you would try to explain the significance of the Industrial Relations Act to them in a face-to-face discussion. Certain people prefer spoken to written messages — probably most of your employees and certainly the less educated ones. Graphical media — posters, charts and the like — tell a story quickly and simply: why not make a point of using them to communicate with your immigrant workers or with unskilled staff? Again, oral instructions are generally easier to understand than written, so why not 'walk the job' every day and *tell* people what you want them to do?

Noticeboards are often handled in a very amateurish way, even when they are management's main channel of communication with the shop floor. Make one person responsible for obtaining authorisation for notices and for posting and removing notices, for nothing kills interest quicker than an overfull board and stale news. Remember that several small boards attract more attention and are easier to keep tidy than a single large board. The correct siting of the board is crucial: nobody will look at it if it is stuck in a dark corner or in the middle of a busy corridor. Give the most important notices the prominent positions. These are, in order: 1. eye level, lefthand side; 2. eye-level, centre and righthand side; 3. top parts of the board. This is known from studying photographs of the eye movements of noticeboard readers.

Telex, teleprinter and telegrams encourage clipped, over-abbreviated messages inherently capable of being misinterpreted, and the use of stereotyped, monosyllabic language. Provided the communicators agree on the precise meanings of these words no harm is done. Thus one firm issues its own 2000-codeword index guide for staff using the teleprinter. One manager, Mr C. H. W. Rhodes, has strong views about the writing of telegrams: 'I really wish that more telegrams opened with a spontaneous phrase such as "Good morning!" How effectively this would exploit the *instant* quality of the medium.' The same manager, writing about house journals, commented: 'I have yet to read a plausible one. Somehow they fail to give a convincing account of life in the company — perhaps because failures and delicate developments such as plant shutdowns are syphoned off the news inputs. The expensive glossies embody centralised anonymity; the grubby photocopies are parochial and dull.' (But vital statistics about the company are not dull to the readers of house journals, although many editors keep them out of their columns.)

Use media in combination

Use the media in varying combinations to achieve different kinds of impact. By using a combination of media you gain the characteristic strengths of each.

Suppose you have to communicate a complicated message about a new bonus scheme to the entire force of 2,000 employees. Your only chance of getting the message through to all of them is to use a number of media in combination. Everybody is allergic to some media but nobody is deaf and blind to them all. Use them in combination so that the people you miss with the first shot you hit with the second. Both groups are then alerted for later messages. You will miss some people with your notice board bulletin but reach them with your Tannoy announcement or when you hold your departmental meeting. Think before communicating. Take the trouble to draw up a media plan: it might look something like this:

1. *Use Tannoy* for alerting the work force to a change of bonus arrangements. Tannoy offers you instant works coverage and everyone gets the message at the same time, thus killing rumour. Give outline information only because this is a low-fidelity medium and only suitable for relaying short, simple messages.
2. *Use memos* to take your message in greater detail into different departments. Each memo points up the aspects most relevant to that particular unit.
3. *Arrange section and departmental meetings* where the details already given in writing can be expanded and clarified. Questions can be answered, complaints noted for action.
4. *Use posters* during the following weeks to remind employees about key aspects of the change and about any actions you want them to take.

You used Tannoy because it is good for getting a simple message to the entire work force simultaneously. You used memos to point up the local significance and particular aspects of the new scheme. You arranged face-to-face discussions because these are the most effective way of answering questions and removing doubts. And posters are good for their reminder value.

Notice the importance of choosing the right *sequence* of media. Tannoy has to precede the memos and meetings – it would be quite superfluous if it came later.

Correct sequence is important. Various channels impinge on people in certain typical sequences. Coleman and others, 1963, have shown that a doctor's first contact with a new drug tends to be via an advertisement in a professional journal while later, additional information comes orally from professional colleagues.

The new London Stock Exchange applies the combination-of-media principle in its permanent exhibition where suspended display panels with batteries of ear phones offer a condensed background in five languages. Simultaneously, a 22-channel display monitors current market price movements while a multi-screen presentation shows the Stock Exchange's role in the life of the country. The new building's telephone exchange allows full intercommunication between all 174 London stockbroking firms and the outside world. Instant contact with dealers is made possible by the pocket paging system – one of the largest and fastest anywhere. Quicker still is the two-way UHF radio system which some firms are using to talk direct to their staff on the floor – the time saved may be only two or three minutes but they can be vital.

US Army research shows that visual presentations of information are more effective than oral but that a combination of both is more than three times as effective as either. Backing up an oral presentation with a written is an effective way of getting your message to the work force.

An American survey questioned company presidents about the most effective ways of communicating very important messages. The presidents strongly preferred oral methods. The following order of preference emerged: 1. explain in a meeting of management personnel, 2. explain in personal interviews with key managers, 3. Issue a management bulletin, 4. memo, 5. telephone and intercom.

The most effective method of all would be to use a combination of all these methods. In practice, of course, these principles can't always be applied. Practical consideration – especially cost – often forces managers to choose second or third-best media and methods.

Telephone

Many people get their first impression of your company over the telephone. Goodwill can be won or lost in seconds. That is why it is important to use the instrument efficiently. In the first place consider what the instrument does to the voice, adding brittleness and brusqueness, making a businesslike speaker sound aggressive. Why not arrange voice training for telephonists and secretaries and so reduce the chances of callers getting a wrong impression?

The telephone instrument itself is only a kind of end-organ enabling us to make use of millions of pounds worth of complex communications equipment. But think of how that end-organ subtly shapes the message it transmits. It crudifies messages because of the lack of all visual clues as to what the other man is feeling and thinking; thus what is said and agreed should always be confirmed in writing so that haziness disappears. Again, the telephone is a purposive medium. You make your call to say something specific or to ask a specific question. You begin by saying what you are ringing about and end by reaching a definite conclusion or making an agreement. Nigel Walmsley has pointed out[1] that people drift into and out of 'live' conversation but not in telephone conversations. Moreover, because of costs and work pressure, telephone calls are usually kept short. *So to get the most out of a telephone conversation prior formulation of the message is needed and a careful selection of material and language. You need to plan your telephone talk and mentally rehearse it in advance.* Exploit the strengths of the medium by following this procedure:

1. Before making the call make sure that all documents, files etc. to which you may need to refer are there in front of you.
2. Make brief notes of what you want to say so that your message gets through quickly and clearly.
3. Make notes of all important points made by the other person.
4. At the end of the call summarise any agreements made and say whether or not you will confirm in writing.

Don't dally over the phone. Telephone talk is tighter, less discursive, more organised than live conversation. It tends to be more clipped and businesslike. These are the characteristics which should be exploited.

Computer

The computer is widely used in industry to find optimum solutions for problems once dealt with by rule of thumb. The computer enabled half a million people to work together with split-second accuracy and timing

[1] In 'The Telephone Act' in *Twentieth Century*, Second, 1968.

on the Apollo moon programme. A computer at Edinburgh University read a large part of the *Iliad* in just 3½ seconds and made a reverse index in a minute and a half — tasks that would have taken a man ten years. The computer allows limitless amounts of information to be stored indefinitely and then retrieved at the touch of a button.

The computer is highly numerate but it is illiterate. It can't deal with value, only with quantity. It can't work out for itself what is important or valuable. It doesn't know when it is being stupid: one computer sent a summons to the mother of a woman aged 106 for keeping the child away from school — it didn't realise that people's ages can run into three digits. Questions have to be put to it in a special way to suit its cold humourless mind. It fatuously quantifies factors which are not quantifiable. It can churn out masses of data about a town but it can never tell you what that town is like to live in.

Even the elimination-of-clerical-drudgery argument has been overplayed. One travel firm had to increase its staff from 70 to 130 after installing a computer. Overheads doubled. The machine was cumbrous and slow — especially in dealing with clients' alterations to holiday plans.

Television

Use closed-circuit television to talk to employees you would never otherwise meet personally. Television allows a single personality to be projected very strongly. For the unique strength of the medium is the intimacy it creates[1], the illusion of close contact between distant people. Don't speak on television as you would on a public platform. On television a loud voice, 'oratory' and a flamboyant manner look absurdly out of place. Television is the medium for the very private person and the very private manner.

Use the medium, as Ford Motors do, as an aid to communication between departments. And remember the many possible industrial applications. For instance, British Rail use it for studying the behaviour of rolling stock under actual service conditions. It allows steelworkers to watch red hot steel being rolled from a safe distance. Hundreds of companies use CCTV for training purposes — for developing inter-

---

[1] According to McLuhan television is not a visual medium at all but an audio-tactile medium: an electron beam scans the image like fingers scanning a line of braille.

viewing techniques and so on. When the videotape is played back the trainee gets instant correction or reinforcement of his method.

CCTV has many advantages over film. It doesn't need projection or processing facilities, the results can be studied instantly, and it is far cheaper. And the equipment itself is fairly cheap to buy – though the skills of production are not so cheap to buy and it is wise to start in a small way until adequate operating experience has been built up.

Screen size limits the number of uses of television. It can't deal effectively with 'big' subjects, such as a large crowd, a landscape, a seascape. Don't record the works annual dance on videotape. Think of how the interest drains away when cinema epics are presented on television. Using the medium effectively implies using many close-ups and avoiding wide, long shots.

Another limitation is the crudity of the television picture. Its 600 lines of electric corduroy blur the image, cut through small details. And the medium doesn't tolerate high degrees of contrast – small objects are either dazzled out or shaded out of the picture. Television colour is extremely crude, too. If you want the public to see exactly how you make lace or embroidery or mount your gemstones, or wish them to appreciate the wonders of microcircuitry, you would avoid television and rely instead on film or still photographs.

The medium is greedy for movement – frequent cross-cutting, scene changes etc. This is because the crudity of the picture and the small screen rule out any compensatory interest in the *detail* of the image. Thus, when a BBC camera team reports life on the cease-fire line it brings back pictures of women screaming at troops, guerrillas practising grenade-throwing. It's great television and it actually happened but, as Julian Critchley has pointed out, balance and contrast are missing. *Inactivity* is the most important aspect of life in the area, but that has been left out because it can't be shown *in action*. Similarly, serious discussions become contests, with the interviewer throwing provocative questions and highlighting the differences so as to provoke the *action* which television must have. No medium this for the subtle insight, the shade of meaning – they don't move. Heroes have to be seen to be heroes, fighting the enemy and carrying the girl to freedom.

Film

Making films is very expensive, but copies can be produced cheaply and, if they are good enough, sold at a profit. The Post Office sold four films to a national distributor and so made an overall profit.

Film is invaluable for many training purposes. A simple loop film can be used to show new operatives a complicated machine operation over and over again: they pick up the techniques far more quickly this way than by traditional training methods.

Don't waste expensive minutes of your film showing stills or moving heads. If stills suit your purpose use photographs or slides. If you only want moving heads why not use the much cheaper videotape?

The strength of the medium is its great precision and accuracy. The nature of photographic emulsion permits very high-fidelity reproduction. This, together with the big screen, allows minute detail to be captured so that film can afford to linger and needn't be as greedy for action as television. Film is the best medium to use if you wish to show the public how you cut your industrial diamonds. But the big screen can also deal with big subjects – use it to show the vast scale of your operations or plant site, the size of your transport fleet, and so on.

Excellent results can be obtained through editing. Ten or twenty or thirty hours of film can be cut into a final version of an hour or less. Many short separate shots can be included, each one technically perfect. What emerges is probably faster and intenser than reality, but it communicates your message with great impact. The physical circumstances in which the film is seen add to the intense effect: people sitting together in the dark, their attention riveted on the bright screen, their emotions roused by the music and effects. When the furnace door flings open your eyes hurt with the sudden glare, you can almost feel the heat. And, as David Riesman has pointed out: 'It can force us to identify with its chosen moods and people. The camera, by moving around, subtly invites us to embrace one character and exclude another; to look up and feel awe of a hero or fear of a villain; to look down and feel contempt or pity. A, sidelong glance at the camera alerts us for trouble.'[1]

Radio

Radio is an intense and private medium. It involves you deeply. You can project into it your fantasies and emotions: there is no image to contradict them. With your transistor you are alone in a crowd. The radio speaker frowns or smiles whenever you want him to. He's talking

[1] David Riesman, 'Gunpowder of the mind', *Atlantic Monthly,* vol. 200, no. 6 December 1957, p. 128.

to millions but he's talking to you alone. A good radio thriller or ghost story is a deliciously petrifying experience because you can project your wildest fantasies into it. Radio triggers off strong emotions and so is a powerful medium for political and religious broadcasting. McLuhan says radio killed off political oratory because you can't orate into a mike. But McLuhan is wrong. You *can* orate into a radio mike because radio permits the illusion of vast distance and space and vast crowds. When we listen to Hitler's voice being broadcast we are in the middle of a huge crowd. Television killed the orator because the image shatters illusions of space and distance.

Radio is little used in industry but no doubt as applications and improvements filter down from the US space programme its importance will grow. Pocket radio telephones can now be obtained which permit the user to dial into private telephone exchanges from a distance of up to ten miles. This could be an invaluable communication aid for salesmen, construction site managers and so on. Many taxi firms use car phones operating on radio waves, and two-way radio sets are used in some firms for keeping in touch with security guards, commissionaires and others. Radio-paging systems are becoming popular — for instance, in hospitals where they provide a fast and reliable method of locating doctors and other staff in cases of emergency.

When using radio for speech the choice of speaker is important. People spin fantastic portraits out of voices and would be quite capable of converting your gruff-voiced chairman into a white-slaver or racketeer.[1] Keep the lisper and the droner away from the microphone. A famous Oxford don was never allowed to broadcast by the BBC because 'they say I squeak'.

Print

Television is groupy, film is public, print is private. Print can explore better than any other medium ideas and emotions and arguments. Speech is loose and spontaneous: print is heavily organised and structured. The speaker can change his position mid-sentence, introduce

---

[1] Harvard researchers found that more than 80 per cent of radio audiences attribute definite physical and temperamental traits to speakers on the basis of voice alone. And T. H. Pear found that audiences even make assumptions about such details as the speaker's height, weight and whether he's extrovert or introvert.

a last-second qualification. But the writer needs to have the whole sentence – or even the whole argument – planned in his head before he writes the first word. *Using print forces analytical thinking and a planned and orderly presentation of ideas, just as film and television, with their cross-cutting and montage effects, discourage these qualities. Print is a good medium for putting across a complex 'case'. It is the medium for advocacy and argument. A major problem though is to find a style and a vocabulary which will communicate to* all *the readers.*

The influence of the mass media

'The year-old Seventy Crusade originating in Dortmund in Germany makes electronic history as it flashes to 36 cities of Europe from Norway to Yugoslavia on closed-circuit TV network. Telephone land-lines carry the Gospel above the Arctic Circle and radio beams it all over Siberia, India and Africa' (Billy Graham)

The mass media have fanned out across the world, bringing Good News to the remotest tribes and regions. But is their influence as powerful as we sometimes think? They are regularly blamed for the ills of society, for destroying culture, creating violence, producing conformity – but with what justification?

Many studies show that the mass media are powerless to alter beliefs and behaviour except in trivial ways. For instance, they seem to have little influence over voting behaviour in general elections. They can influence us to change in trivial ways, but, even then, only indirectly: television may attract our attention to a new hair style or fashion trend but most of us wait for somebody with high prestige from our own neighbourhood to endorse the new fashion before adopting it ourselves; 'Ideas often seem to flow *from* radio and print *to* opinion leaders and *from them* to the less active sections of the population.'[1]

According to Joseph Klapper and other experts, the mass media operate conservatively, reinforcing rather than changing our ideas; following public opinion and taste rather than moulding it. People don't expose themselves to the media in a state of psychological nudity. They come clothed in their prejudices which influence both *selection* of programmes and *perception*, so·that we tend to see in a message which

---

[1] See E. Katz and P. F Lazarsfeld, *Personal Influence*, New York, Free Press, 1964, p. 32.

challenges our beliefs confirmation of them. Perhaps the mass media are more effective in creating opinion about new issues where there are no existing positions to be defended. We can't be got at in any profound way – this is what Hugh Cudlipp meant when he said, 'A newspaper may accelerate but never reverse the popular attitude which common-sense has commended to the public.' Perhaps the real power of the mass media lies in their ability to determine not what we think but what we think about by creating 'consensus': 'They tie together the many pluralistic face-to-face groups in which attitudes are formed. They bring certain common issues to the attention of all of them ... place the current issues of politics on the agenda of citizen discussion.'[1]

In backward parts of the world perhaps they have a more radical influence. When David Lerner studied the effect of the new mass media in the Middle East he found that in many villages the man with the radio or the young bus driver who'd seen movies in the capital and could bring back news of the great world was ousting the village elders from positions of influence and leadership.

Points to remember

1. Use the media to express what they are good at expressing. Create a swift, sharp-etched impression of a person with television. Search that person's inner world with print. Report an operation on his eye with film. Change his attitudes by involving him in group discussion.
2. Use the company media in combinations, so that the people you miss with the first shot you hit with the second. Both groups are then alerted for later messages.
3. Use company mass media to consolidate *information* already transmitted via line channels. Remember that mass media – e.g. the house journal – are relatively powerless to alter beliefs and behaviour.
4. Some subjects lend themselves to visual presentation – e.g. to explain a new plant or factory design to your employees you would use a model or drawing. Graphical media such as charts and posters tell a story quickly and simply: why not use them systematically for communicating with unskilled or immigrant workers?

[1] See I. de Sola Pool, 'The Effect of Communication of Voting Behaviour', in *The Science of Human Communication,* ed. W. Schramm, Basic Books, 1963.

5. Oral instructions are generally easier to understand than written. So why not 'walk the job' every day and *tell* people what you want them to do?

6. Backing up an oral presentation with a written is an effective way of getting your message to the work force. US Army research shows that visual presentations of information are more effective than oral but that a combination of both is more than three times as effective as either.

7. The telephone instrument adds brusqueness and brittleness to a voice, makes a businesslike voice sound aggressive. Why not arrange voice training for telephonists and secretaries and so reduce the chance of callers getting the wrong impression?

8. The telephone crudifies messages because of a lack of all visual clues as to what the other man is feeling and thinking. Thus what is said and agreed should be confirmed in writing so that haziness disappears.

9. Use closed-circuit television, as Ford Motors do, as an aid to communication between departments. And use it for training purposes – e.g. training people in interviewing techniques. Play-back gives the trainees immediate consolidation or correction of their techniques.

10. Film is invaluable for many training purposes. For instance, a simple loop film can be used to show new operatives a complicated machine operation over and over again. They pick up the techniques far more quickly this way than by traditional training methods.

14 How To Streamline Your Information System

'The answer is in there — somewhere!'

Information is the raw material of sound management. Decisions and policies are made out of it. It can mean the difference between expansion and stagnation. Indeed, information failure can kill a company: misinformation about the costs of an engine plunged Rolls Royce into bankruptcy. But too much information can be as dangerous as too little. Superfluous information chokes communication channels and bewilders the decision-makers. The individual manager who finds himself snowed under with information needs to develop coping techniques — such as those outlined here.

Management is the process of converting information into action. Managers without adequate information have to rely on precedent or memory when taking action. While the road is dead straight you can drive by looking in the driving mirror; but you go off the road at the first unexpected turn. At times of rapid change old methods lose their effectiveness. At such times, failures of information are more dangerous than lapses of control. As Harold Wilensky has pointed out, the latter may bring rapid decline but the former can mean sudden death. Rolls Royce survived many labour relations crises but misinformation about the costs of an engine plunged the company into bankruptcy. The Japanese government clearly recognises the value of up-to-date information: it has set up a department which reads every technical journal published in the world.

High-quality information is the essential raw material from which good decisions are woven. Useless, low-quality information only chokes communication channels and slows down the administrative machine. High-quality information is accurate, clear, timely and, above all, relevant to one's job. How much of the information that you receive has these characteristics?

By never relying on a single source some executives safeguard against having to use low-quality information. Roosevelt checked and balanced information from official sources against information from his own unofficial and highly unorthodox sources. He used one informant's information to balance and check on another's. Many managers practise this method. Several subordinates are set to work independently to collect the same body of information or to assess the same problem and

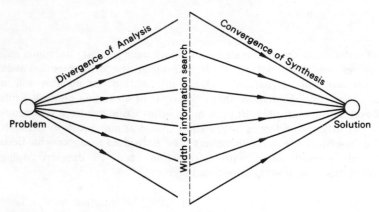

Fig. 31: *This diagram indicates the crucial role played by information-search in solving problems. Generally, the wider the search the more focused and accurate the solution. But there are many risks involved in making wide searches — eg cost, overload, delays, and the emergence of contradictory blocks of evidence.*

172

the results are then carefully compared. When the subordinates only learn what is going on through a third party the effects on morale can be shattering — as I know from personal experience.

One reason why so much low-quality information lands on your desk is that in modern industry data are easy to obtain and cheap to process.[1] How often have you stared at a pile of computer print-out and said, 'The answer is in there — somewhere', then decided not to make the effort of searching? To stop this happening one computer firm is developing techniques for answering *specific* questions only instead of supplying masses of routine print-out relating to a problem in a very *general* way. Specific answers to specific questions are distilled from a mass of collected statistics and sent to the manager within twenty-four hours. This firm realises that quality of information is more important than quantity.

Don't assume that the more information you have about a problem the better your decision will be. First, it is hardly ever possible to assemble enough information to remove *all* doubts about a decision. Secondly, the greater the bulk of information assembled the greater the chance of different blocks of information implying different decisions. This creates confusion and finally forces the manager to accept one part only and reject the rest. In an unpublished paper Dr J. Schermer has observed that high-risk decision-makers make their decisions as soon as they have enough information to indicate a *fair* chance of correctness while conservative decision-makers wait until they have enough information to indicate a *very good* chance of correctness. Whether a firm adopts a high-risk or low-risk policy depends partly on what is at stake and partly on the temperaments of the top managers.

Computers

As the organisation expands the number of decisions increases yet there is often less time in which to make them. That is why an up-to-date information system can mean the difference between stagnation and

---

[1] The concept of information as something that can be moved about and precisely measured and stored stems from Shannon and Weaver's *The Mathematical Theory of Communication.* The number of 'bits' that must be assembled to answer a particular question comprises the amount of information to be processed. Shannon and Weaver's theory was to guide communications engineers in their design of equipment but it is often applied to the general problems of communication in industry.

expansion in a company. Fortunately the growing complexity of business problems has coincided with the development of technological tools for handling them. Information can be assembled and processed today on a scale never possible before. The computer can take the guesswork out of decisions and improve planning and organisation by producing masses of information at the right time: by massive and instantaneous information exchanges it can tie together all parts of a huge, scattered organisation.

The efficiency of computers seems to depend on individual managers asking the right questions, for information is good, bad or indifferent depending on the relevance of the questions asked. The machine itself will go on spewing out useless data until somebody tells it to stop. A great deal of useless information will be eliminated when computers can construct programmes for themselves. As Norton Bedford has pointed out, this will be possible when the decision-making process itself is better understood, when rules for deciding how to act can be fed into the machine. Thus future generations of computers may well take over the *higher* levels of managerial activity.

Fig. 32: *Below the clutter of routine circulars, sales leaflets, unsolicited reports, promotional gimmicks etc. a few useful facts lie hidden. But every item added to the pile makes them harder to get at. Some system is needed to separate the useful from the useless.*

The main test, I suppose, of a computer's usefulness to a company is whether it works for or against the people in the company. Is it creating or reducing information overload? Does it give managers more or less time for face-to-face contact? Is it producing high-quality information or masses of useless print-out? Can it keep a secret?

The secrecy problem seems to be causing growing concern. Any modern government holds a great deal of information about every individual. It would be easy to link it all in a central data bank for all departments to draw on as required. It would be easier still to add court and health records. The Younger Committee, which inquired into secrecy, suggested that information should be regarded as held for a specific purpose only and not used for other purposes; and that 'in computerised systems handling information for statistical purposes, adequate provision should be made in their design and programmes for separating identities from the rest of the data'. Industry would do well to adopt these general principles.

Information overload

Information is the lifeblood of sound management: decisions and policies are made out of it. Everyone recognises the danger of too little information flowing in a company. But too much information can be just as real a danger, bewildering the decision-makers, slowing down the

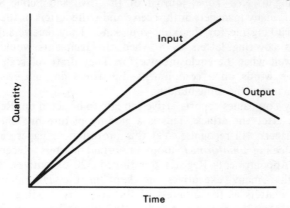

Fig. 33: *As information input increases, the manager reaches then passes his point of peak efficiency. As more and more paper piles up on his desk inefficiency and confusion begin to appear.*

175

administrative machine. Think of the papers lying on your desk at this moment. Probably some contain useful information, some are irrelevant to your job while others will never get read – but all have cost time and money to produce. Information is vital for efficiency, but as Sir Paul Chambers, ex-Chairman of ICI pointed out: 'The best system of information is that achieved with the least paperwork.'

Some managers assume that a full and free flow of information is somehow good for productivity and morale. But consider the experience of the United Sound and Signal Company. In this company, people were kept so well informed that the point was reached where, as one executive put it, 'virtually everybody knows everything that is going on while it is still materialising'. Middle managers began to complain about being snowed under by information about day-to-day operations with which they were not directly concerned. Communication channels became blocked by low-quality information which made it difficult for high-quality information to get through.

In many companies managers receive masses of information that they can't possibly use. Forms, memos, circulars, reports flutter down on to their desks like autumn leaves. They clutter up desks and drawers. They divert the manager from more important work such as planning and policy-making. And the volume tends to grow, for paperwork breeds paperwork. More and more people are needed to deal with the deluge. Efficiency sags as the office turns into a papermill.

According to *Red Tape*, journal of the Civil and Public Services Association, many managers both receive and write letters of the 'thank you for thanking me for thanking you' kind. They receive and write superfluous covering letters even when the recipients would know perfectly well what the enclosure was for. They draft full-scale letters where three words on a compliment slip would do, and even write letters to rooms in the same building.

In many companies reports arrive too late to be acted on. Red alerts flash days after the attack. This is a gloomy picture but one which many managers will recognise. Yet this profusion of paper can leave managers feeling *uninformed* about important matters. Recently the Graduate Appointments Register questioned 320 executives. Answers revealed that many executives are kept in the dark about such important matters as the progress of the company, trading prospects and profits. And the report concludes: 'It is the feeling of professional and serious-minded executives that their companies are unnecessarily reluctant to trust them with more information.' Yet how many of these executives feel snowed under by masses of *useless* information?

Overload is perhaps more of a problem in large, complex organisations than in smaller firms. Large organisations have denser networks of communication than small. As organisations grow the need for information increases at a disproportionate rate. To a certain extent, indeed, conditions of overload are quite normal. All firms have certain average constancies of production and fluctuations from these inevitably cause overload or underload at various points in the system: an industrial dispute temporarily overloads the production manager with messages. But when managers become *permanently* overloaded with information the problem becomes serious.

The technological means of generating information have rapidly developed while the individual's ability to handle the increased flow has stood still. Thus higher management often becomes so overloaded with information that it can make no real use of it. Management Information Systems become Management Misinformation Systems. Too much communication is bad communication.

The kind of problems created by overload can be more easily grasped by looking at the analogy of what happens when an electronic amplifier circuit is subjected to too strong a signal, thus creating an overload. A number of effects are possible: 1. distortion of signal; 2. saturation in output, i.e. no matter how the input signal is increased beyond a particular point there is no further increase in output; 3. breakdown of one or more components in the amplifier. The electrical engineer deals with the overload either by attenuation of the input signal or by modifying the circuitry so that it can cope with an increased signal. Similarly, the manager can deal with overload either by reducing the flow of information or by making certain structural reforms.

Coping procedures

In *The Social Psychology of Organisations* Katz and Kahn have described typical responses to an overload situation. These include:

· *Over-simple decisions.* The number of decisions made increases but the quality of decisions drops.
· *Omission*, causing problems to magnify: the complaint which is ignored may finish up in court.
· *Error.*
· *Queueing.* Incoming information has to wait its turn for processing.
· *Approximation* — a blanket way of responding.

· *Selection* of certain kinds of information only for action. Or processing only those parts of a message which are easily understood.

Many people in industry are well aware of these problems. One consultant thinks that inessential information would automatically be cut out by treating information as a commercial product with the government paying companies for form-filling and industry buying information from government and other agencies at the market rate.

But usually the people who complain most about surplus information (and complaints seem to grow louder with seniority) are the very people who should act to stop it flowing. How often do *you* make a point of going to talk to your employees rather than sending them written messages? How often do you ask yourself, when about to send a memo, Is this really necessary? Many managers never even get round to working out what information they need and what they can do without; they simply carry on with the paperwork they inherited. But any manager can draw up plans for his own departmental Management Information System and apply his ideas within the narrow limits of his own command. Of course, this would require a systematic study to determine the information needs of different types of employee. Generally, requirements vary between different occupational groups and at different levels: for instance, skilled men require different content *and form* of information from unskilled men.

Could you boost the efficiency of your department by applying any of the following ideas?

1. *Set up a special section for screening incoming communications.* Masses of information arrive by letter, phone, memo, telex. . . . Some is irrelevant, some could be condensed, some needs sending back for amplification. One company head has estimated that of all the external information that comes into the company, 90 per cent should be sorted out before reaching him, and that it is essential for him to see only about 1 per cent of the total. The responsibilities of the section could include:

· speeding important messages to senior managers
· destroying all irrelevant information – sales leaflets, PR handouts and the like. One company cut the amount of filing in the general office in half simply by destroying all incoming acknowledgements and covering letters.

· making digests of wordy documents and technical reports and sending the condensed versions only to personnel who really need them. The United Sound and Signal Company found that employees required *detailed* information about their own sections or specialisms but only *summarised* information about other sections, general company policies etc.

· sending minutes of meetings to carefully selected personnel.

2. *Set up review machinery to root out all unnecessary forms, records and procedures.* Sometimes paperwork is necessary only because more effective administrative techniques are lacking. The review body could be authorised

· to scrap minor records (paper-clip issues etc.)
· to veto unnecessary procedures (cheque endorsements etc.)
· to ban or redesign forms: could headings and instructions be simplified? Are multiple copies really necessary? Marks and Spencer stopped literally tons of paper flowing by such simple devices as scrapping unnecessary forms, abolishing time records and simplifying stock requisitions.
· to remove names from circulation lists.

3. *Update filing and storage systems.* Trim down fat files and so clear the way for faster information retrieval. Microfilm can get rid of acres of paper; it allows reduction in the ratio of 150:1. Given an efficient index, information stored on microfilm is easy to locate and retrieve.

Consider building into your new filing system a procedure for destroying records as they become obsolete. You could, for instance, use a simple colour code: red = destroy on 1 January; blue = destroy on 1 July etc.

4. *Delegate paperwork.* For instance, routine reports could be sent to a junior who would read them through, pass on important points, and destroy or file the rest. Encourage subordinates to send you *short* reports: these will give you the information needed for decision-making in an easy-to-use form.

5. *Consider moving personnel to fit into the work-flow* and so reduce the physical movement of paper about the department. Investigate

Reducing Overload

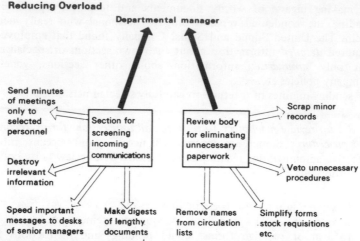

Fig. 34: *Overload can be reduced by setting up the appropriate administrative machinery.*

air-tube systems and other methods of moving papers by mechanical means.

Methods like these have proved their value in many British companies. Each organisation needs its own custom-built system. But all systems should have one quality in common: adaptability. For as an organisation grows and becomes more complex its parts interlock more completely. Thus changes in one department affect all the others and the company is in a state of constant organisational flux. This makes continual revision of the information system necessary.

One executive has hit on his own private method of dealing with overload:

The first technique is that the pile of papers on your desk, which always seems to be growing, is *sifted through every morning* and the interesting ones selected for processing. The development of this technique is to *keep a list of matters outstanding* and review this each morning rather than the pile. When doing this I personally find it difficult to decide on priorities. Should one tackle the short unimportant job required by this afternoon or the long important job due next month? Other managers I know allow a pile to accumulate but rather than review it regularly they put in date

Inefficient seating arrangement   **Efficient seating arrangement**

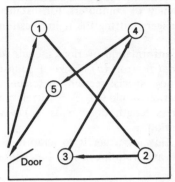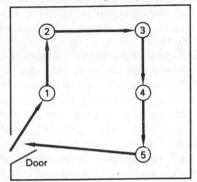

Fig. 35: *Illogical seating arrangements increase the physical distance that paper has to travel.*

markers and do nothing until someone raises the matter again, when it is retrieved from the pile and brought to the top. If it has not been raised again in three months' time it is thrown away. When they have nothing else to do they process the pile on the LIFO (Last In First Out) principle.[1]

Develop your own coping techniques and don't be a victim of communication overkill! Remember that simplicity is the essential quality of any information system. The sort of system that requires a whole army of employees to handle procedures for eliminating procedures is logically absurd.

Reminders

1. At times of rapid change failures of information are more dangerous than lapses of control: the latter may bring rapid decline but the former can bring sudden death.
2. Masses of low-quality information block communication channels and bewilder the decision-makers. High-quality information is accurate, clear, timely and relevant: it is the raw material from which good decisions are woven.

[1] The author, Mr Colin Pearson, is a systems analyst working for ICL.

3. Information is good, bad or indifferent depending on the relevance of the questions asked. The efficiency of computers, for instance, seems to depend on individual managers putting the right questions to them.
4. Typical responses to a situation of information overload include (*a*) over-simple decisions, (*b*) omission, (*c*) error, (*d*) blanket response.
5. To reduce overload, why not set up a special section for screening incoming communications? The section would (*a*) destroy irrelevant information, (*b*) edit and compress length documents, (*c*) send selected items to managers for attention.
6. An effective way of reducing the flow of paper is to scrap minor records, simplify or abolish forms, and veto inessential procedures such as cheque endorsements.
7. Microfilm allows reduction of documents in the ratio of 150:1. Yet with an efficient index rapid retrieval is possible.
8. Any information system should be *simple to operate* but also *adaptable* so that it can be modified to cope with future changes of structure or environment.

15 Communication Barriers

'The ancestral hunting pack in grey-flannel suits.'

Communication barriers exist in every organisation – between managers and workers, between professional and technical staff, between different departments and between different occupational groups within departments. People misunderstand and mistrust each other because of different responsibilities, backgrounds and goals. Some of these barriers are inbuilt and not much can be done about them. (For instance, specialisation is essential in a large organisation yet it creates formidable communication problems.) Other barriers can be overcome if there is sufficient determination and knowhow.

In any company there are numerous communication gaps. Managers are separated from their employees because of different codes of conduct and frames of reference. There are gaps between departments: each department thinks it is the most important and finds it genuinely difficult to appreciate the contribution of the others. There are gaps between experts in different disciplines, between professional and technical staff, between branches and headquarters. You can never assume that your own group's norms and expectations and vocabulary are the same as those of the group next door. People interpret messages and react to them in different ways, according to their positions in the organisation. *Thus a good knowledge of the social system of the organisation and of how particular individuals fit into it is essential for accurate communication.*

In specialist departments where communication consists largely of technical information flowing between like-minded experts communication can be rich and accurate because sustained contact and similar training and experience have given the communicators similar terms of reference. Communication can be full and accurate because the individuals understand each other. The problems begin as the message proliferates. As it spreads across departments and levels it becomes increasingly fragmented and distorted because of the lack of common reference points.

In large organisations it is especially difficult to achieve accurate communication. Patterns of communication tend to be complex, and blockages or distortions ('noise') can occur at numerous junctures. The problem was highlighted in an ILO report on industrial communication which pointed out that the more complex the organisation, the more detailed are the steps which management must take to ensure that information reaches all parts of the organisation and that information from all parts of the organisation is fed back to itself.

In large organisations, *physical* distance between units and *psychological* distance between specialists and different levels cause numerous communication breakdowns:

Sources of failure are legion: even if the initial message is accurate, clear, timely and relevant, it may be translated, condensed or completely blocked by personnel standing betwen the sender and the intended receiver; it may get through in distorted form. If the receiver is in a position to use the message, he may screen it out because it does not fit his preconceptions, because it has come through a suspicious or poorly regarded channel, because it is embedded in piles of inaccurate or useless messages ... or simply because too many messages are transmitted to him (information overload).[1]

[1] See H. L. Wilensky, *Organisational Intelligence: Knowledge and policy in government and industry*, (Basic Books), 1967, p. 41.

The classic problem of departments or branches 'covering up' takes root: the department head, faced with falling production, hunts round for exonorating reasons and builds his report round these. And with the proliferation of experts the jargon problem grows. The walled-in specialist writes reports that only he can understand. Meetings with members drawn from many different units and disciplines, achieve a high decibel-count and a true non-meeting of minds.

In a large organisation *hierarchy* causes distortion and the strangling of upward communication; and *centralisation* severs local experts and managers from the decision-makers and so encourages irrelevant and misleading information. Communication failures are, in a sense, built into a large and complex organisation:

> In so far as the proper mastery of the task calls for specialisation and the need to motivate and control personnel necessitates hierarchy; insofar as coordination demands centralisation; ... in so far as internal security and outside competition necessitate secrecy ... a singleminded attention to administrative reforms that facilitate the flow of accurate information is inappropriate.[1]

Wilensky goes on to refer to some possible remedial actions: if a hierarchy is tall, flatten it; give more experts more autonomy by having them report to fewer bosses; set up interdepartmental task forces to overcome departmental blockages; use secrecy only where functionally necessary.

The Communication Process

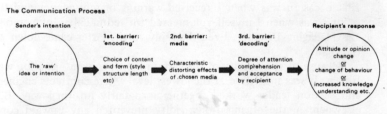

Fig. 36: *There are inbuilt barriers within the communication process itself. They stand, as it were, between the communicator and the response he is trying to evoke in the recipient. To communicate effectively you have to a) select relevant material and present it clearly and unambiguously b) choose the best media for the job c) attract and maintain the recipient's attention d) make sure the message is comprehensible and acceptable.*

[1] *Ibid.*, p. 179.

Another useful tactic for improving matters is to simplify communication networks within your own area of command. For instance, you could rationalise the work-flow to ensure that fewer people are involved in handling any particular piece of production or administration. Another device is to reduce the number of supervisory levels in your department or unit thus eliminating a number of the relay points at which the message can get blocked or twisted. The fewer people between sender and receiver the more accurate the message. Where possible, go direct.

Poor upward communication

Good upward communication gives managers the information they need for sound decision-making. It brings the employees' on-line experience to bear on company problems and acts as a kind of early warning system about shop-floor problems and grievances. Why then is upward communication so inadequate in so many firms? One reason is the lack of listening ability in many top managers, which is often linked with an over-reliance on formal channels for feeding information upwards:

> Adherence to the 'line' communication system was very strict and only occasionally did the individual contracts engineers by-pass their section leaders. On only two occasions in the three years of my employment there did I have any direct contact with the MD: the first occasion was when I received warning of redundancy and the second was when I myself volunteered for redundancy by memo to the Managing Director. Even the reply to the latter came down via the chain.
>
> Because of the rigidity of the system the flow of information was frozen. It was most free at the lowest level where contracts engineer and section leader worked together in a fairly informal way. But elsewhere in the organisation rigidity prevented any upward communication taking place except where it was specifically requested.
>
> The contracts manager attempted to promote informality by exchanging a friendly greeting on the corridor. His stock phrase was, 'Are you well?' He never listened for a reply and this became the office joke.

The writer, J. Fenton, is a highly qualified engineer. Yet his employers seem not to have been interested in his ideas. Very many employees would endorse his observations. *The inability to listen at top level strangles the desire to tell at lower levels.*

How well do *you* listen?

Do you listen to your subordinates hard enough?
• Do you have enough personal contact with employees and their representatives? Do you know enough about them – their goals, values, abilities? Do you try to learn their point of view?
• Do you hold enough meetings with employees to discuss their problems and grievances?
• Do you use communication methods appreciated by employees? For instance, do you use the shop steward as an important channel of upward communication?
• Do you regularly check that foremen are passing upwards information, ideas, grievances received from below?
• Do you know about the occupational and the informal groups which individual employees belong to? About the values and methods of these groups and the relations between them? And about how the individuals fit into them – the status structure?

The kind of controlled communication which is implied by these questions eats up valuable time. But far more time can be spent sorting out the misunderstandings and grievances that arise when the upward communication flow becomes choked by neglect.

How to stimulate upward communication

Most of us tell the boss what we think will please him. We feel we can't afford to expose our failures and weaknesses. In a study of fifty-two managers, Read found that men on the way up tend to restrict information about their problems because they want to please the boss and preserve comfortable work routines. As a result, bugs in the system multiply.

Why not consider adapting some of the following techniques for stimulating upward communication for use in your own company?

1. *Set up a special section,* within the Personnel Department, say, to collect information about employee attitudes and grievances. The information could be collected by anonymous questionnaire or by confidential interviews then sent direct to top management for use in policy-making.

2. *Confidential exit interviews* would help you to discover workers' *real* reasons for leaving and perhaps reveal serious shortcomings in the organisation.
3. *Using an employee counsellor* can have the double effect of boosting morale on the shop floor and revealing grievances before they become storm centres.
4. *Informal get-togethers*, such as morning coffee conferences, can greatly stimulate upward communication within the management team.
5. *Polaroid Corporation employees can phone a special number* and state their grievance or question. Answers are sent direct to the employee then printed in the company newspaper. In other companies there are certain times when top executives are available for phone calls from employees on any topic.
6. Suggestion schemes are used almost exclusively for ideas about technical improvements. Why not widen the scope of the company's suggestion scheme and *encourage suggestions about plans, policy, and managerial methods* and relay all these suggestions direct to the board?
7. *Train all managers in the mechanics of information gathering and editing.*

In-fighting

Everyone who has worked in a large organisation has experienced the aggressions, tensions and anxieties that infiltrate every workshop and office. Seen from this angle, the organisation is a battlefield where individuals and cliques emerge and fight each other for status and power; and where the knives are out waiting for the backs to turn. Fierce in-fighting erupts in every nook and cranny. Perhaps conflict of this kind is unavoidable, even a biological principle. The ancestral hunting-pack in grey flannel suits.

The relevance of this to the communicator is that as messages fly to and fro across the battlefield they get torn and distorted. A dislikes B so sends a deliberately misleading message, or says only what must be said and not one word more. B distrusts A so reads into his message all sorts of hidden threats and twisted motives.

In many companies the left hand never knows what the right hand is doing. It probably doesn't know what the left hand is doing. How well do people understand their own emotions?

One way of opening people's eyes to their own blindness is to arrange a sensitivity training course. Managers from different units are assembled and split into two groups. Each group presents a case to the other requesting some action — the release of certain statistics, let's say. Each group discusses the other's request. The discussions are taped and the tapes played back and analysed in terms of the amount of heat generated. Each side then describes how it viewed the other's motives, how it misinterpreted and misconceived, and describes the emotions it felt. Gradually the participants become aware of their own distorting aggressions and fears, which affect the way they see and communicate with others in the organisation.

You read with your feelings

People don't perceive the real thing. Facts become festooned with fantasy. In one experiment boys had to estimate the sizes of piles of coins. The greater the value of the coins the greater their overestimate of the size of the piles. They didn't, however, overestimate the size of a pile of coin-shaped pieces of cork. The tendency to overestimate was greater in the poorer children.

Feelings can shrink a message. Karen Horney has observed how anxious people who feel under a threat actually observe less than when they are not feeling threatened. A man who is afraid of being made redundant may miss the point or not register part of your argument if you send him a reassuring memo.

Feelings can play tricks on your memory so that you vividly remember parts of the message but completely forget the rest. Rapoport reviewed experiments showing that pleasant material is remembered longer than unpleasant material. Sharp showed that acceptable phrases such as 'securing justice' were remembered longer than unacceptable phrases such as 'fearing poison'.

The Rorschach ink-blot test and other projective devices show that people project their own schemata on to what they see and hear. Into every message they read their own romance. Thus the same simple message changes its meaning as it passes from hand to hand. Schramm has observed that at one stage in the communication process the message is merely ink on paper or reflected light waves or rarefactions in the air — and a sign can only have such meaning as the observer's experience permits him to read into it.

An incomplete or poorly worded message in particular invites people to use their imaginations to work it out. Consider this simple memo: 'After stopping the machine please check that safety guards are secure.' To one man this may mean: 'I've been noticing how carelessly you operate your machine.' To another it may mean: 'Don't knock off work early again or you'll be sorry!' And to a third: 'I know I can rely on you to do the right thing.' *To reduce the chances of your messages being twisted in this way, why not pause for a moment before sending the message out: try to anticipate the possible ways in which the message might be misinterpreted so that you can make a point of stating that's not the meaning that should be read into it.*

Group pressures can distort judgment. Asch studied college students' judgment of different professions. When told the other 500 students rated politics highest the subject tended to raise his own evaluation of the profession. In another famous experiment, 123 subjects were asked to say which of three lines was the same length as a standard line after five stooges had unanimously given a wrong judgment: 37 per cent were wrong compared with less than 1 per cent normally.

These are just some of the factors which conspire to twist even the simplest message as it passes up or down the line. In a large firm where there may be seven or eight levels between the Managing Director and the shop floor, a message can undergo a complete shift of meaning as it is relayed downwards.

'Translating' messages

A person interprets a message in terms of his own frame of reference. Where this differs from the sender's, misunderstanding creeps in. Sending a message in the same basic English to all recipients is not good communication if everybody who reads it interprets it differently. *To reduce the chances of mutliple interpretation you may need to 'translate' your message into several different 'languages' so that each group will understand it and respond to it in the way you intend. You may need to use several small communication loops instead of a single, all-embracing loop: stilettos rather than the club.*

Suppose you have to communicate details of new holiday arrangements to everybody in your department. At first you think of pinning up a notice on the noticeboard for all to see: a single large communication loop. Then you remember that the last time you did this some of your supervisors complained about not being informed in advance of the general announcement. You also recall that some of your immigrant cleaners recently complained about not being able to understand the difficult language of many noticeboard announcements. So you decide to use a number of small communication loops and to send several memos:

1. *A memo for supervisors*, to be handed to each man personally several days in advance of the general announcement. Full reasons for the change to be given.
2. *A memo for operatives*, to be posted on the central noticeboard a few days later and giving brief reasons for the change.
3. *A memo for the cleaners*, to be pinned up in the cleaners' tea room and written in very plain language and explaining very simply what action must be taken and who to go to for further explanation.

Down go three potential communication barriers! And this approach also solves problems of correct timing – i.e. making sure that people receive the message at the required time and in the right sequence.

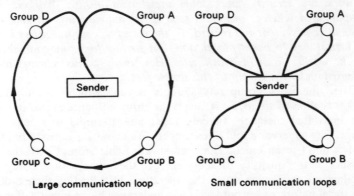

Large communication loop   Small communication loops

Fig. 37: *Small communication loops allow quick circulation of the message and rapid feedback. They also enable the sender to 'translate' his messages into 'languages' preferred by different groups, and to use a variety of media according to the differing needs of the recipients.*

Using small loops and 'translating' messages in this way is necessary because different levels and different groups talk their own occupational and social jargons, and see things in different ways. Dearborn and Simon gave twenty-three managers a long case history of a company to study. When asked to identify the major problem of the company 83

191

per cent of the sales executives said it was a sales problem, 80 per cent of the production managers identified it as a production problem, and so on. What each man sees as the facts of the case depends largely on his position in the organisation, and you need to take account of this tendency when communicating with him.

Them and Us

Managers and workers have generally been to different schools. They live in different parts of town, go to different pubs, rarely mix socially. Neither learns the other's point of view. How many communication breakdowns in industry spring from this experience gap? Perhaps nationwide comprehensive education would be the best long-term method of improving industrial relations in Britain.

No wonder that so many management announcements filled with words like efficiency, productivity, profitability, fall on deaf ears: managers are committed to these values whereas the workers' main aims at work are security and stable social relationships. Workers are group-minded whereas managers tend to be individualists striving for personal achievement and reward. To the manager, cash incentives seem the logical way to boost production. But striving for money might cut off the worker from his workmates. How many bonus schemes have collapsed under the weight of this simple fact?

Often the work group sets a quota beyond which no individual worker is allowed to go. So strong is the group influence in this respect that individual members fiercely resist any attempts to change its norms. One supervisor told a researcher: 'We know our time studies for welders don't mean much. They can always fiddle around with the air pressure or the quantity of acetylene ... they always find a way of speeding up or slowing down the operations by adjusting their tools.' The social nature of output levels was underlined by an investigation in a relay assembly plant which showed that girls tended to work at the same speed as their friends. The manager needs to be aware of the cleavage in social ethics that separates him from his employees, and desist from making individualist appeals to employees to boost their production or improve their timekeeping.

Restriction of output

Consider the problem of output restriction. To the worker the practice is a completely logical way of protecting himself against unreasonable demands or possible redundancies, and any attempts by management to convince individuals to the contrary are fiercely resisted. Operatives will change their methods and raise their output only when the group as a whole nods its approval. To break through this particular barrier, call the group together and explain why the change is necessary; offer new forms of security for old (e.g. guarantee jobs and earnings); then leave them to *talk themselves* into a change of attitude. Only in this way can the emotional barriers be overcome. Such an approach carries risks: if the discussion leads to a hardening of attitudes and a refusal to change there is nothing you can do about it.

Sometimes you need to let employees make their own decisions. Bavelas compared two groups of sewing machine operators in the Harwood Company. One group was allowed to discuss and decide its own production goals. The other group made no decisions and set no goals. *This group failed to improve its performance, whereas the first group boosted its production because it had decided to. Through participation management can increase its control by seeming to relinquish it.*

An experiment was carried out in a toy factory where girls had complained about the speed of a moving belt carrying components for assembly. After discussions a control dial was fitted to the work bench so that the girls themselves could control the speed of the belt. The girls were very pleased and morale soared. And the average speed at which the girls themselves ran the belt was higher than the speed they had complained about.

Participation can release hidden springs of energy and encourage employees to accept change. And that is a valuable effect. For change itself is the only constant in modern industry.

Participating

Henry Ford was touring a new automated engine factory with Walter Reuther, President of the Auto-Workers' Union. When Ford remarked to Reuther, 'Walter, these machines never go on strike', Reuther replied, 'True, but they don't buy any automobiles either.' If you think about it, Reuther's reply contains a sufficient reason for treating workers and their representatives with a special kind of courtesy and respect – the kind that would have seemed soft-headed a generation ago. One Managing Director at a motor components factory wouldn't agree with that proposition. When the union official called to talk about the case of a dismissed foreman the Managing Director sent a curt message saying he was too busy to see him. Next day the official made four phone calls only to be told each time that the MD wasn't available. So every foreman in the factory came out on strike in protest. Moral: avoid high-handedness — it doesn't pay.

Times have changed and workers have changed. Employees are better educated, more sophisticated than they were a few decades ago. The development of automation and electronics has caused a shift from craft skills to numerical control with a consequent blurring of white- and blue-collar distinctions. Employees are better equipped than they used to be to contribute to company plans and policies. Vic Feather, former Secretary of the TUC, has said that he'd like to see workers discussing such matters as manpower requirements, delivery dates, new machinery and other matters still widely considered to be the exclusive prerogative of management.

Many managers still jib at the thought of introducing wideranging consultative processes, fearing that to do so would be to relinquish some of their powers. Perhaps they are right. Perhaps each extra piece of participation machinery represents a real transfer of authority. But perhaps too the most formidable communication barriers in British industry can only be overcome by this kind of radical transformation. No doubt participation is easier to introduce in relatively new companies where patterns of power and influence are not deeply engrained.

A powerful braking force on the trend towards decision-sharing is the undemocratic nature of most companies in Britain. The votes that control them go to money not people; the running is done by a small and powerful group; power rests at the apex. No doubt in time company law will be reformed to increase managerial accountability and to bring the voices of the employees into the board rooms. Such a transformation is long overdue for there are countless areas where the experience of the man on the job can do much to improve methods and efficiency. As Mary Parker Follett pointed out half a century ago, the man who works with the machine is as expert about it in his way as the man who designs or the man who buys the machine. This is the assumption at Parish Instruments where informal meetings are held on the factory floor during protracted tea breaks: company plans and problems are discussed with the Managing Director joining in.

At Rowan Engineering the staff decide most matters in the company. For instance, they elect managers and foremen and even fix their salaries. Matters of policy are decided on by all employees. The factory is run by its members. This approach has relieved the company of severe financial problems. At Scott Bader, job applicants are interviewed by some of the people they will be working over. While in the Computer Management group all levels have identical desks, the same carpet and the same amount of space. The Managing Director, in the middle of a large, open-space office, can be freely approached by any employee; as a result of this free communication many problem areas have been revealed. Details of salaries are kept in an open file accessible to all, and employees can use 10 per cent of their salaries to buy shares in the company. One of the company's founders said: 'We are like an army with only officers — the computer is our only private soldier.'

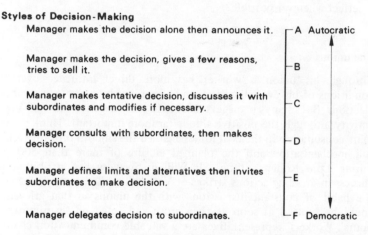

Styles of Decision-Making

Manager makes the decision alone then announces it. — A Autocratic

Manager makes the decision, gives a few reasons, tries to sell it. — B

Manager makes tentative decision, discusses it with subordinates and modifies if necessary. — C

Manager consults with subordinates, then makes decision. — D

Manager defines limits and alternatives then invites subordinates to make decision. — E

Manager delegates decision to subordinates. — F Democratic

Fig. 38: *Even in firms where there is no formal participation machinery managers consult their subordinates informally about job problems. Joint decision-making is good for training subordinates and also for facilitating change, A survey of 166 senior managers by Frank Heller* shows that style D, above, is more frequently used in decision-making than any other (37%), The survey also revealed that the more important decisions were likely to be made by autocratic methods.*
*Reported in Managerial Decision-making, 1971.

Participation checklist

1. If participation exists in your firm is it experienced at every level?

2. Do employees get the information they need in order to participate effectively?
3. Is participation used merely as a manipulative device to win support for decisions already made by management?
4. Are employees allowed to participate only in decisions which don't hurt management?
5. Within the last five years has the company devised any new joint consultation machinery or extended bargaining processes?
6. Do workers share any gains from increased productivity resulting from participation?
7. Has participation led to increased feelings of satisfaction among workers?
8. Are recommendations made by consultative committees put into effect wherever possible?

The unions

Through his union a worker has more direct influence over the conditions of his everyday life than he exercises by his vote at a general election. But many managers see only the negative side of union activity although the positive side is far more important. Think of how joint consultation in the coal mines enabled the smooth introduction of full mechanisation and the planned closure of more than 500 pits during Lord Robens's time. Sir William Swallow has attributed his success in avoiding serious strikes at Vauxhall while he was its head to the habit of constant discussions with the unions so that grievances could be spotted as soon as they arose and acted on 'in minutes or hours'. Workers' representatives are a valuable communication channel for conveying information and feelings both upwards and downwards and for explaining management's plans and policies to the work force. The modern union boss talks about wages and prices in terms indistinguishable from those used by the CBI. Management and the unions are partners in industry if only they would acknowledge the fact.

Professor Tom Lupton has shown that even the disruptive side of union activity can serve a positive purpose. The entire trade union machinery of strikes, ballots, go-slows etc. acts as a kind of battering ram, smashing down barriers, forcing management to listen and to make necessary changes, clearing the ground for realistic policies.

Key points

1. People interpret messages and react to them in different ways, according to their positions in the organisation. Thus a good knowledge of the social system of the organisation and of how particular individuals fit into it is essential for accurate communication.

2. The fewer people between sender and receiver the more accurate the message. Reducing the number of supervisory levels in a firm can improve communication by eliminating some of the relay points at which messages get blocked and twisted.

3. Do you stimulate upward communication by seeking personal contact with employees and their representatives? Do you know enough about them — their goals, values, abilities?

4. A useful device for stimulating upward communication is to set up a special section to collect information, by questionnaire or interview, about employee attitudes and grievances. The information can then be sent to top management for use in policy-making.

5. Feelings can shrink a message: if you send a man who is afraid of becoming redundant a reassuring message he may register only a part of the message. Feelings also play tricks on memory; for instance, the receiver may remember the pleasant parts of the message and forget the unpleasant parts.

6. People project their own schemata on to what they see and hear so that the same simple message changes its meaning as it passes from hand to hand. Try to anticipate the possible misinterpretations so that you can make a point of stating that that is *not* the way it should be interpreted.

7. To reduce the chances of multiple interpretation, it may be necessary to 'translate' a message into several 'languages' so that each group understands it and responds to it in the way you intend.

8. The most effective way of overcoming output restriction is to call the work group together, explain why a change of standard is necessary, then leave them to *talk themselves* into a change of attitude.

16 Getting Your Message Through to People

'Start with a bang when the audience needs to be roused.'

As well as the mere mechanics of communication, the manager needs to know how to ensure that his messages are noticed and remembered. He needs to know how to convince people and to engineer the required response. One of the manager's many roles is that of professional persuader. Some of the skills needed to fulfil that role are outlined here.

An article appears in the house magazine of an engineering firm. Written by the Personnel Director, it makes out a strong case for setting up a new type of consultative committee. The idea is promptly thrown out by the unions as a piece of management manipulation.

In a plastics factory a noticeboard bulletin announces a simple change of clocking-on procedure. Employees somehow read into the notice a warning of future redundancies and they threaten a walkout.

Every manager with experience of handling a large work-force knows how suddenly and inexplicably this kind of communication breakdown can happen; how easily simple messages get twisted and distorted. That is why every manager needs to know more than the mere mechanics of communication. He also needs to know how to get through to people, how to talk to them in their own kind of language, how to convince them: he needs to be a communicator.

Business communication harnesses theory and makes it serve practical ends. It's an engine to make the wheels go round. Individual communications are effective not for any stylistic reasons but because they are easy to understand, produce the right response, convince people, get the job done. You compose a bulletin carefully, express it in faultless English and pin it on the noticeboard. But 20 per cent of your employees never read it, 20 per cent fail to understand it, and most of the rest misinterpret it. So you fail to communicate. Mastery of the *mechanics* of communication is no guarantee that communication will happen.

The manager as persuader

Management training programmes in the future will surely have to pay greater attention to basic communication skills. For speaking and writing skills can be powerful agents of persuasion and control, and that is what management is all about. Many managers are suspicious of what they regard as the manipulative techniques of the persuader but perhaps their fears are exaggerated. For the same knowledge that increases the manager's persuasive powers also increases the scepticism and critical faculties of the employees. Although the modern manager is a professional persuader he is in a race to keep up with the growing resistance of his employees.[1]

Boosting retention

Within three days people forget about 80 per cent of what they read. But if they read the message and also hear it they only forget about 35 per cent. Repeating the message and using a variety of media greatly

---

[1] It must be admitted, though, that the potentiality for persuasion is growing and that some of the developments are frightening. By planting electrodes in a dog's brain and pushing buttons you can make it do almost anything. It sometimes seems as if the common schizophrenic delusion of thought-control could come true.

Sending messages upwards	Sending messages downwards
1 Information for higher levels needs to be GENERAL rather than PARTICULAR — broad in scope with the detail eliminated. Thus a report or memo for higher management usually needs to be backed up with an interview for clarification and a filling-in of the background.	Information for lower levels needs to be PARTICULAR rather than GENERAL. Thus, as directives and instructions from top management pass down the line they have to be expanded, filled out and 'translated' to suit the needs of each group. One effect of this is frequent distortion of the message.
2 The message needs to be arranged so that its relevance to policy-making is immediately apparent. Thus financial implications, effects on turnover, overheads etc. need highlighting. This increases the value of the communication as a decision-making tool.	The message needs to be arranged so that its precise relevance to the recipient is spelled out. Each man needs to know exactly what is required **of him**. Remember that general instructions have to be applied to more and more situations, level by level, until eventually they reach the man on the shop floor or in the saleroom who must **act** on them.
3 Usually the **financial** aspects need to be thoroughly explored, with conclusions adequately supported by reliable evidence.	Usually precise **technical** information is required so that operatives, for instance, can produce exactly the part required, with the precise specifications, clearances etc.
4 *Examples of useful information:* — summary of total demands on production over a six months' period. — summarised quarterly results from each department. *Less useful:* — a mass of 'raw' sales figures. — detailed maintenance costs, week by week, section by section.	*Examples of useful information:* — for salesmen, a detailed description of a new product with full operating instructions: for adding to their order sheets. — for operatives, precise specifications for machining a new piece of equipment. *Less useful:* — the technological principles involved in a new production process. — a history of the management-union negotiations as an introduction to an announcement of a new pension scheme.

Fig. 39:

increases retention. Krueger found that repeating the main points of a message increases retention. Jersild found that retention improves up to three or four repetitions (with little extra improvement for further repetitions). Hollingworth concluded that (*a*) repetition of the message, and (*b*) variations in style, form and expression together increase retention. All these research findings have the same practical implication: *you improve the chances of your message being remembered by repeating it, by varying the media used, and by varying the form – style, layout etc. Repetition and variation of form also improve the sharpness with which the message is remembered: by repeating the same message in different words or in a different form any ambiguity or uncertainty is eliminated.*

Perhaps the mechanism at work is that rehearsal and repetition tend to organise many separate items into a single pattern or unit in the mind thus reducing the load that the memory must carry.

Thus a sensible way of communicating an important change of policy might be (*a*) to announce the change at a meeting, (*b*) to confirm the announcement by a noticeboard bulletin, (*c*) to publish full details of the change in the house magazine. Repetition and variation drive the message home.

Regard a communication as a ball in a skittle game. Usually you can knock down more skittles with three or four shots than with a single ball.

Fig. 40: *People tend to be 'visualisers' or 'verbalisers'. Thus you may need to present the same information both verbally and visually. Use signs, symbols and pictures to supplement words and create faster understanding.*

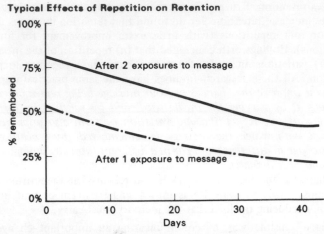

Fig. 41: *Repeating the message improves retention until a saturation point is reached — sometimes after as few as four or five repetitions. An advertising agency found that after seeing an advertisement once 14% of the housewives surveyed could recall it. But after seeing the advertisement 13 times during 13 weeks, 63% could recall it successfully. Of course, retention scores depend partly on the method of measurement chosen.* For instance, conclusions are generally better remembered than details.

Arrangement of material

Which part of a communication or series of communications has the greatest impact — the beginning, the end or some intermediate part? Where should you place your strongest, the most important and interesting, material — at the beginning or at the end of the communication? Investigators have been trying to answer these questions for half a century or more and, generally speaking, have produced contradictory results. For instance, Luchins gave subjects two contradictory descriptions of the same person. Whichever description was read *first* overwhelmingly dominated the impression formed when subjects met the person. Cromwell found that the *last* of a number of speeches caused the greatest amount of opinion-change. All researchers, however, agree that material placed at *intermediate* points is the most difficult to remember. For example, Hovland found that with lists of three-letter syllables the middle parts of the list were the hardest to remember.

The primacy—recency riddle has no clearcut answer. So the

following guidelines are offered tentatively and only as a basis for experiment and discussion.

Place 'strong' material (important and interesting points) at the beginning when the audience is likely to be 'cold' and needs to be roused and motivated to read or listen to your message. Thus a sales or advertising message needs to start with a bang. In cases such as this, lead with your ace and arrange material in order of decreasing importance and interest.

Place strong material at the end when the audience will probably begin reading or listening with interest but is likely to become bored or fatigued before the end. This might happen, for instance, if you posted up a notice about a new and complicated bonus scheme or overtime arrangements: the employee would begin reading with great interest but perhaps become tired before reaching the end. The best tactic would be to encourage him to stay tuned in by progressively scaling up the rewards — i.e. reserve the most interesting points for the last sections of the communication, after telling your readers early in the communication that you will be dealing with these interesting points later.

Trustworthy communicators

Why is one manager accepted by the work force while another meets only with suspicion and hostility? Why do employees sometimes accept the arguments of the shop steward while rejecting what their managers say? A famous experiment suggests some answers to these questions. Two groups of students were given the same statement to read about an industrial dispute. One group believed the story came from the *New York Times*. The other group was told it came from the *New York Daily Worker*. The first group thought it was fair and objective; the second group rated it unfair and one-sided.

With every message comes an important cue — the knowledge of *who* said it. This knowledge helps us to decide whether to accept the message, reject it, regard it with suspicion and so on. A communicator who is judged *trustworthy* — expert, experienced, unbiased etc. — can produce three times as much opinion change as an untrustworthy communicator (Hovland and Weiss, 1951).[1] Employees accept what the

---

[1] Normal criteria for judging trustworthiness are abandoned in abnormal situations. Bettelheim described how prisoners in a German concentration camp were so influenced by their guards that they imitated their appearance and enforced rules long since forgotten by the guards themselves.

shop steward tells them when they trust him. Manager A has more influence over the work force than Manager B because he is trusted and so more credible. *Perhaps one way of improving company communication would be to adjust selection methods so that managers and supervisors are selected because they have the ability to inspire trust in their subordinates.*

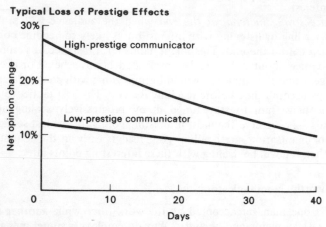

Typical Loss of Prestige Effects

Net opinion change

High-prestige communicator

Low-prestige communicator

Days

Fig. 42: *After 30 days or so the loss of prestige effect of a 'trustworthy' communicator is almost complete,* and the opinion-change that remains is probably the result of message-content. Thus high-prestige communicators are most effective when an immediate action or commitment is required — an instant decision or vote or purchase.

Typically, in joint negotiations each side sees the other as biased and one-sided. Each side distrusts the opposing side and so closes its mind to the other's case. Sometimes the result is deadlock. In such a case, why not call in an independent outside chairman? His comments and assessments of each side's case would be 'heard' on both sides of the table, seep through the mental filters, because he would be seen as an impartial observer and therefore trustworthy. Mutual understanding would grow; the deadlock might be broken. This is one of the few cases where communication through a third party is more rewarding than communicating direct.

When the communicator is seen as having something to gain from influencing his audience his trustworthiness and therefore his persuasiveness go down. Two research men gave the same speech on devaluation to different audiences. One man was introduced as a 'university economist' and the other as 'head of an import company'. The 'university man' was judged more objective and to have made a better job of his speech than the company head, who was perceived as having something to gain from influencing his audience. Equally, the manager who is seen as having something to gain (status, promotion etc.) from influencing his employees to accept a wage offer, let's say, to that extent becomes less capable of persuading them. Again, a house magazine article about the benefits of a new profit-sharing scheme will have more impact if written by a reputable outside figure than by the Managing Director.

But even low-credibility communicators usually produce a change of opinion in the recommended direction. Presumably the positive impact of the message content is greater than the negative impact of the communicator.

Persuasive types

The least sophisticated people are the ones most open to persuasion.[1] The Opinion Research Corporation has recommended political communicators to identify the persuadable and ignore more resistant sections; and to make their appeals as *direct and simple* as possible, since the persuadable group contains a large proportion of the less sophisticated voters. A subtler approach is needed with more sophisticated audiences. For instance, a two-sided or all-round approach to controversial subjects often has the greatest impact, perhaps because it implies honesty and objectivity. A completely different tactic is required when you are trying to persuade a single person: Meldman and Lanckton, 1970, found that when two people are trying to persuade each other the winner tends to be the one who most expresses confidence in his own case and throws most doubt on the other person's. Yet refutations of an *audience's* arguments only arouse *resistance* to persuasion (Thistlethwaite, Kamenetzky and Schmidt, 1956).

---

[1] According to Lazarsfeld, persuadable types tend to be depressive and socially inadequate and to have low self-esteem. On the other hand the most resistant types include the very aggressive and neurotic.

Group discussion

The more important an idea is to a person the more fiercely he resists any attempt to change it. His first line of defence is to expose himself only to messages which tend to support his prejudice. And even if a challenging message does get through he can escape unscathed by a kind of motivated missing of the point. This explains why the mass media have far more power to reinforce opinions than to change them.

The most effective way of breaking through the prejudice barrier is to use the weapon of group discussion. When Lewin tried to persuade American housewives to change their food-buying habits during the war he found this method far more effective than speeches, lectures and other methods. Lewin's own conclusion was that 'if the group standard itself is changed the resistance which is due to the relation between individual and group standards is eliminated'. Individuals are unwilling to depart too far from group standards as every manager who has encountered output restriction will know. But individuals will change their ideas and their ways radically provided the group changes.

People have to be allowed to talk themselves into a change of attitude. A roughly similar mechanism seems to operate in psychotherapy, which is more effective in its results when the patient draws his own conclusions about his attitudes and behaviour. Why not tackle the problem of slack time-keeping by allowing employees to discuss the advantages and disadvantages of punctuality; or by allowing them to discuss and fix their own starting and finishing times? Awkward individuals will feel the pressure to conform to the new group standards.

Five ways to add impact to your message

1. *Know your objective.* The more precise this knowledge is, the surer your control of events and the more accurately you can word your message.
2. *Identify your audience.* A particular audience may require a special kind of language: talking computers to computer men requires one kind of language, talking computers to chemists requires another. Your audience may be so diverse that you may need to use several kinds of language; or no language at all.
3. *Choose appropriate media.* Take into account the size of the audience, speed required, cost and characteristics (see chapter 13).

4. *Check timing and sequence.* Precisely when should the message be transmitted? When should it be received? How can you make sure that accurate timing is achieved? Who should get the message first, who second, and so on?

5. *Encourage feedback* if the message is important. This will enable you to deal with problems, correct misunderstandings and check that the message has been received and acted on.

Piercing the din

Managers need to know more than the mere mechanics of communication. They also need to know how to get their communications through to the people who are sitting entrenched behind their emotional barriers. For people don't receive messages in a state of psychological nudity. Their opinions and prejudices wrap them in a protective clothing; and once they distrust the communicator no amount of clever talk will persuade them to accept his arguments. When confidence and trust drain away there is resistance, not change.

As well as emotional filters there are also perceptual and mental obstacles to effective communication. These can prevent your employees understanding or remembering a message. They may even prevent them noticing it in the first place. That is why a knowledge of the ideas outlined above or, better still, a willingness to experiment with them and adapt them, can add strength and clarity to your voice and give it a better chance of being heard above the surrounding din.

Reminders

1. Mastery of the *mechanics* of communication is no guarantee that communication will happen. A well-written memo is useless if most of your employees misinterpret it or refuse to comply with it.

2. Within days, people forget nine-tenths of a message they have seen or heard only once. To boost retention (*a*) repeat the message, (*b*) vary the media used, and (*c*) vary the form of the message (layout, words used etc.).

3. Information coming at the beginning or end of a communication is better remembered than information occurring at intermediate points.

4. Place strong, interesting material at the beginning of a communication when the audience needs to be roused and motivated to see or listen to the message. For instance, a sales or advertising message has to start with a bang.

5. Trustworthy communicators are more influential than untrustworthy communicators. One way of improving company communication is to start appointing managers and supervisors on the basis of their ability to inspire trust in their subordinates.

6. Sometimes in negotiations a deadlock situation can be broken by bringing in an outside chairman. Because both sides trust him they 'hear' his comments and assessments of each other's case. Thus mutual understanding increases.

7. Simple, direct appeals work well with unsophisticated audiences. More sophisticated audiences respond favourably to subtler methods — e.g. a two-sided or all-round approach to a controversial subject.

8. When two individuals are trying to persuade each other the winner tends to be the one who most expresses confidence in his own case and throws most doubt on that of the other person.

9. The company mass media are powerless to change employee attitudes. The only way to break through the prejudice barrier is to use the weapon of group discussion.

10. To add impact to your message (*a*) know your objective, (*b*) identify your audience, (*c*) choose appropriate media, (*d*) check timing and sequence, (*e*) encourage feedback.

APPENDIX 1
The Conference Business

Accustomed as they are to public speaking, conference delegates soon become terribly bored unless the entire event is smoothly organised and stylishly staged. A bad hotel, poor food and service, a draughty, inconvenient hall – any of these can ruin the event.

At one time you could lock up your delegates for days on end in some dreary hall and tell them tedious things they wished they'd never heard of. But not any more. Today most companies take care with their conferences, seeing them as a valuable means of building morale and corporate pride. Thus one company recently opted to hold its annual conference in a French château. Island conferences held in Cyprus, Madeira, Majorca, are increasingly popular. One London company will set your conference in any European capital and include first-class hotel, a reception and sightseeing from about £150 a head.

Many important conferences are now handled by professionals and stage-managed throughout, with edited speeches, professional lighting and several rehearsals of the entire proceedings to ensure pinpoint timing. Masters of this art are the American political parties. The 1972 Republican convention was a meticulously scripted affair. A BBC reporter came across one of the scripts. It laid down the time for speeches, for applause and for spontaneous demonstrations.

At a conference of grocery chiefs Maxwell House presented a musical play set in the Kingdom of Coffee. When Prince Granular wins the hand of Princess Purity the happy outcome is the rattle of tiny coffee beans. The six hundred grocers went home hell-bent on selling coffee by the crate.

The conference industry is big business. A conference of American lawyers held in London in 1971 was worth about £2 million to the capital. Harrogate earns about that much from conferences each year. One London conference bureau has described the kind of conference centre which they reckon is already needed in the capital: a main hall to seat 6,000 delegates and several smaller rooms for smaller sessions of 100, 300, 500 delegates, and so on.

Administrative tips

If you are the luckless one chosen to organise your next conference these few guidelines may help.

1. Don't attempt to handle both accommodation arrangements *and* organisation of conference sessions singlehanded. Enlist the help of a deputy and make him responsible for one of these aspects.

2. Start to plan the conference six to twelve months in advance. (Preliminary plans for one large conference recently held in London were made eight years before.)

3. When planning conference sessions think out everything that is going to happen – chairman introduces speaker, speaker approaches up middle aisle, spotlight on etc. – *and get it down on paper.* This will enable you to brief fully all participants nearer the day. Make a checklist and go through it repeatedly to make sure nothing has been left out. Use it during the conference to ensure smoothness and continuity.

4. Don't rely too much on speakers: even the 'names' can be very disappointing. Use them as a launch-pad for group work. Everybody enjoys himself a lot more when there is plenty of activity and participation – buzz groups, panels, syndicates etc.

5. Make morning sessions long and afternoon sessions short. Give it them while they can take it.

6. At the end of the conference, collect delegates' assessments on an assessment sheet: this feedback will help you to avoid repeating your mistakes next year – if they ask you again.

APPENDIX 2
A Note on Grammar and Punctuation

Today the rules of grammar are generally regarded with less awe than they used to be. Grammar is useful only if adherence to it enables accurate communications to be passed.

Does it really matter if somebody splits his infinitives or uses prepositions to end sentences with? The grammarian, Jespersen, pointed out that nobody would dream of calling 'the good man' a split nominative; and Churchill lambasted the preposition rule as 'arrant pedantry up with which I will not put'.

Punctuation is similarly regarded as a practical aid for helping the reader to grasp your meaning. Hence the general trend to lighter punctuation. The sole exception to this is the full stop which is more frequently used today than ever before because of shorter sentences. Generally speaking, insert a punctuation mark if it aids clarity and leave it out if it doesn't.

Regard the paragraph simply as a device for breaking up a message into readable bits. Always avoid long paragraphs of close-packed type. They have a heavy, eye-repelling look about them.

Use the colon to draw attention to a succeeding quotation, list or explanation: its use in this sentence is an example. Use the semicolon for separating parts of a long sentence: 'During their trip the delegates visited the new smelting plant in the Urals; a recently opened coal mine in Georgia; and several Government economic agencies.'

Use the hyphen for making two separate words into a compound word but, generally, only when this is necessary to avoid ambiguity:

Hyphen needed: 'The scrum-half forgot the rules.'
Hyphen not needed: 'Many problem solving meetings are a waste of time.'

The dash is often used to save the writer the trouble of choosing the precise punctuation mark that is needed. It is frequently used to enclose additional information inserted into the sentence: in most cases, readability would be improved if the additional information were placed in a separate sentence.

APPENDIX 3
Listening at School?

Children listen far more than they read (two-thirds of a child's time at school may be spent listening) and they are more influenced by the things they hear than by what they read. Yet in spite of the palpable importance of listening to a child's development little money and research are spent on it.

One reason for the lack of urgency is the false assumption that good listening comes naturally and requires no training. This is far from the truth. There is much evidence to show that untrained listeners comprehend little and remember far less of what they hear. They are likely to remember no more than 10 per cent of a message they heard three days before.

Studies frequently show that lack of competence in one communication skill hinders growth in the others. There seems to be a sequence in language growth from listening and speaking to reading and finally to writing. Training the child in efficient listening would automatically encourage the other facets. They in turn would strengthen his listening ability.

In other words, the language a child speaks and writes can be no better than the language he listens to (deaf children learn to speak only with special instruction). Therefore, of the four basic communication skills – listening, speaking, reading and writing – listening is the *most* basic. *How many failures of communication in industry result from lack of early training in listening?*

Perhaps the time has come to start squeezing listening skills into school curricula. Admittedly this would bring problems. Few teachers know the techniques for developing listening ability: the teachers would first have to be taught. And scoring and grading procedures and diagnostic tests would have to be developed.

Not just one skill but many skills are involved in listening and all of them would have to be taught. Ruth Strickland has suggested that there are several grades or levels of listening ability:

1. No listening unless directly spoken to.
2. Half-listening while pursuing one's own thoughts.
3. Passive listening with apparent absorption but with little reaction.
4. Responding to speech with items from one's own experience rather than reacting to what is being said.
5. Listening and expressing reactions, through questions and comments, to what is being said.
6. Listening with a genuine meeting of minds.

Few managers ever reach the status of properly developed listeners. Fortunately training can help. And the *earlier* the training the better the results.

INDEX